Supporting Achievers to Unlock Sustainable Career Success

Theory, Strategy and Practice

Carolyn Parry

trotman | t

Supporting Achievers to Unlock Sustainable Career Success

This first edition published in 2026 by Trotman, an imprint of Trotman Indigo Publishing Ltd, 18e Charles Street, Bath BA1 1HX.

© Trotman Indigo Publishing Ltd 2026

Author: Carolyn Parry

British Library Cataloguing in Publication Data
A catalogue record for this book is available from the British Library.

Paperback ISBN 978-1-911724-75-9
eISBN 978-1-911724-76-6

The authorised representative in the EEA is Easy Access System Europe Oü (EAS), Mustamäe tee 50, 10621 Tallinn, Estonia.

Printed and bound in the UK by 4edge Ltd.

All details in this book were correct at the time of going to press. To keep up to date with all the latest news and updates and to access the online resources that accompany this book, use this QR code or visit www.trotman.co.uk/pages/supporting-achievers-to-unlock-sustainable-career-success-resources

DEDICATION

To all the practitioners and professionals who help others to discover their wings and find the courage to fly – please remember to care for your own needs too.

To those who support the supporters, thank you – your care sustains those of us who so often give more than we realise.

And to Rhys, my soul mate – thank you for continuing to encourage me to fly despite facing your own challenges.

Contents

Foreword

As multifaceted individuals, we are shaped by our lived experiences, the situations we face, people we know, our strengths and values, physical and mental attributes and our body chemistry.

Add to this an environment of turbulent economies and rapid technological change, and it is hardly surprising that it can be a challenge to discover and maintain what really makes us happy and fulfilled in our working lives.

It can be all too easy for thieves such as Perfectionism, Comparison, Approval-Seeking, Overwhelm, Depletion, Disconnection and Burnout to rob us of our resilience, fulfilment and career wellbeing. Even people who seem ostensibly to have achieved what they wanted can be susceptible.

In this expertly crafted book, Carolyn Parry shows how she enabled seven achievers to identify and overcome these thieves. Rich in research and references, it provides a guide to each thief, its influence in the workplace and effect on individuals depending on their age, gender, neurodivergence, socio-economic status and cultural and ethnic perspectives.

The sections in each chapter on listening to what each client says and relating this to a wide range of specific theories are enlightening as are the explanations of neuroscience and body chemistry which show how vital it is that action is taken before further damage is done.

The use of models and practical strategies reveals how each client was enabled to see the patterns in their behaviour, reframe their situation and take positive steps towards career wellbeing.

The book concludes with a chapter on the Seven Protection Principles which provide a framework for creating conditions where everyone can flourish without falling prey to the Seven Thieves. In doing so, Carolyn provides hope that by working together as professionals, the personal, social and economic costs of living in rapidly changing times and failing to look after career wellbeing can be overcome.

If you work in career development, careers education, executive coaching or HR, investing time in reading this book will definitely be well spent. You may also find that some of the thieves resonate with your own situation and can then utilise the practical strategies for your own self-care and career wellbeing.

As someone who worked in the career development sector for 40 years, many of which in senior professional roles, I have no hesitation in recommending this book. Its content will inspire and educate you, aid your own professional reflection and enable you to help your clients find their wings and fly off to a life in which they will thrive.

Claire Johnson,
RCDP and CDI, NICEC and ICCI Fellow,
September 2025.

About the author

Carolyn Parry BA (Hons), FRSA, FHEA, FIEEP, FCDI, RCDP

A multi-award-winning career and life coach, TEDx speaker, non-exec director, podcaster and author of her 2023 book, *Change Your Story: Escape from a Job You Hate and Create a Career You Love – On Purpose*, Carolyn Parry is a recent past President, Chair of the Board and Fellow of the Career Development Institute.

Her background as a professional of over 40 years' standing includes a pivotal midlife shift from a successful but soul-eroding 17-year management career across property, international software, and defence and tech publishing into career development work after a period of burnout. She spent almost 15 years at Aberystwyth University, where she progressed from trainee careers adviser to careers and employability director and equality champion, before founding Career Alchemy, her career and life coaching practice, in 2015.

Carolyn specialises in supporting lost and frustrated early/mid-career professionals and executives online through career challenges and change. She is qualified and experienced in a wide range of coaching, therapeutic and stress-related techniques. She uses her own research-proven career change methodology and toolkit called '*INSPiRED*' to help clients gain career clarity and confidence, so they can use more of their potential to enjoy greater fulfilment and achieve more purposefully without burning out.

Her organisational client base includes UK and Welsh Government, university providers including Aberystwyth, USW, UWTSD, Loughborough, Newcastle and NPTC; associations and bodies including the CDI, AGCAS, the QAA, and HELOA; councils including Gwynedd and Lambeth, charities including NESTA and PRIME Cymru, and business organisations including Antur Cymru, Pugh Computers, EY and Unilever.

A member of the Careers Writers Association, her expertise and interests include career change, values, purpose, confidence and motivation; entrepreneurship; the UN Sustainable Development Goals; future-proofing careers against the impact of AI; and, in particular, career wellbeing for high and overachievers. In addition to her careers and life coaching-related qualifications, she is also trained in the use of journalling, Mindfulness-Based Stress Reduction, emotional intelligence, Belbin team role theory and several complementary therapies.

A previous national trainer for members of AGCAS (Association of Graduate Careers Advisory Services), and an Aberystwyth University Learning and Teaching Fellowship and Student Led Learning and Teaching Awards winner, Carolyn was the 2017 recipient of the CDI's UK Careers Adviser/Career Coach of the Year. She went on to receive two business awards for start-up and growth from King Charles while HRH Prince of Wales and was awarded a £20,000 grant from the UK Cabinet Office (No. 10 Downing Street) for career development work with parents and teenagers through 'Careers Advice for Parents', then part of Career Alchemy.

Carolyn has over 20 years' experience as a company director and more than 10 years' experience as a non-executive director. She currently serves as a Trustee Director on the Board of Antur Cymru, a £4M social enterprise that helps rural Welsh businesses start and grow, and, until recently, was also on the Board of Ceredigion Citizens Advice, part of the UK-wide network of Citizens Advice charities.

It is fair to say that Carolyn Parry is an example of an archetypal achiever.

Acknowledgements

When I wrote my first book, *Change Your Story: Escape from a Job You Hate and Create a Career You Love – On Purpose*, I discovered just how many people it took to take it from a concept to a book that really made a difference to people. *Supporting Achievers to Unlock Sustainable Career Success: Theory, Strategy and Practice* is no different.

My first thanks must go to everyone at Trotman for accepting my proposal and helping me to bring it to life. In particular, I would like to thank Alexandra Price, my editor, for her help and positive responses to changes I wanted to make to the structure along the way and her flexibility in adopting a chapter-by-chapter approach rather than receiving it just as one finished manuscript. This book can only make the difference I hope it will if it gets into the hands of as many readers as possible. My thanks here go to Marketing Manager, Claire Lawlor, and Rani Race, Sales and Marketing Assistant, for all their help with this and promoting the book. I also need to thank Louisa Smith, not least for putting up with my interference on the front cover design!

My second set of thanks goes to all my clients who trusted me with their career challenges, enabling me to identify, test and develop the concepts and activities which make up the Seven Thieves framework. Special thanks go to those who allowed me to use their stories in this book to illustrate those concepts in action.

My third set of thanks goes to the kind, helpful and generously supportive career development professionals, careers education specialists and HR practitioners, leaders and consultants. Particular thanks go to Steven Plimmer, Research Manager for the Career Development Institute (CDI) and freelance researcher, for his guidance on how to research quickly to find key themes for exploration and consideration, to Chris Targett RCDP of the career guidance, education and training charity CXK, for his suggestions and encouragement overall and in particular for his wise comments and insights on the neurodivergence content in each of the Seven Thieves chapters. Thanks too to Liz Reece, RCDP and CDI Fellow of Liz Reece Careers, for her encouragement and comments on Chapter 4, to Debbie Dymock, RCDP of Northamptonshire Careers for her enthusiastic and helpful feedback on Chapter 5, to Sharon Evans, Acting Workforce Strategy Implementation Manager at Health Education and Improvement Wales, part of NHS Wales, for her encouragement and helping me to make a stodgy theory section much more appealing, and to Kathryn Robson,

Chartered MCIPD, Chief Executive of Adult Learning Wales for her helpful suggestions from an HR perspective for Chapter 7.

There is one other career development professional I need to thank – Claire Johnson, RCDP and CDI, NICEC and ICCI Fellow, CDI Board member and the CDI's original Head of Professional Development and Standards. Claire was incredibly diligent and helpful in reviewing every chapter for me, was my unwavering cheerleader throughout the book and suggested an extra step which turned the original 5Ds activity in Chapter 5 into the 6Ds exercise. I owe her a massive debt of gratitude – and definitely some gin!

My final thanks must go to Rhys, my husband of almost four decades, who for the last 25 years has had to put up with having an achiever wife who is passionate about the power and impact of the career development sector and never stops talking about it.

Diolch o galon – thank you all. Without you, this book would not have been possible.

Mid Wales, September 2025.

Introduction and how to use this book

The growth of an achievement culture

As practitioners, we only need to spend a few minutes scrolling through LinkedIn or other social media platforms to see today's achievement culture in action. Every day, millions of individuals showcase their personal brand by posting awards, promotions and success stories – content often fuelled by the rise of social selling. Yet these polished narratives frequently conceal an underlying existential vulnerability, a mask that is beginning to slip.

In 2017, Curran and Hill conducted a large-scale study exploring cultural shifts and rising perfectionism among college students across 27 years. They identified three societal trends that underpin the achievement culture we now inhabit:

- **Competitive individualism and neoliberalism:** In modern capitalist societies, individual success, self-improvement and personal branding are treated as personal duties. Failure is internalised, and perfectionism becomes a way to remain competitive and avoid falling behind.
- **Meritocracy:** Schools, universities and workplaces place significant weight on grades, rankings, job titles and performance indicators. Worth is "earned" through constant achievement, fuelling both self-driven striving and external pressure to appear flawless.
- **Parental pressure:** Competition seeps into family life, where anxious and conditional parenting ties approval and acceptance to performance. Children learn that respect must be earned, embedding perfectionistic thinking from an early age.

Alongside these cultural shifts, the very concept of career has evolved. Lifespans are lengthening, and with shrinking demographics, career lifespans are also likely to extend further. At the same time, the definition of career has broadened. The Career Development

Institute (CDI) describes it as *"the lifelong, unique process for each individual of managing learning, work, and transitions in order to move toward an evolving preferred future and participate effectively in work and society."* Significantly, its definition links career development not only to personal and economic wellbeing, but also to productivity and social justice.

Career success, happiness and achievement

In our rapidly changing, technologically driven economy, careers have shifted from the traditional "job for life" to more fluid patterns – gig work, career pivots, side hustles, digital nomad lifestyles, influencer roles and portfolio careers. The COVID pandemic added a collective pause, prompting widespread reflection on what success and happiness mean individually and accelerating new patterns of hybrid and home-based working.

For younger generations, purpose and fulfilment have become central. Millennials and Gen Z often prioritise impact and learning over security, recognising that home ownership and pensions may be out of reach in the current economic climate. Meanwhile, the rapid adoption of generative AI has transformed organisations' expectations of productivity, not only augmenting human work but also intensifying pressure to adapt and perform. This is likely to increase the number of professionals seeking careers support as AI-led disruption reconfigures sectors, causing new roles to emerge while others become obsolete.

This backdrop of continual change collides with our human drive to pursue happiness and success "perfectly," amplifying the vulnerability Curran and Hill identified. Rising burnout, mental health challenges, sickness absence and disengagement are evidence of this tension, as we see later in this book.

Given these dynamics, it becomes essential to examine the relationship between success and happiness. Success is most commonly defined as the accomplishment of meaningful, usually linear goals and markers, encompassing both external achievements (income, promotions, recognition) and internal fulfilment (purpose, contribution). Happiness, by contrast, is best understood as a sustained state of wellbeing that combines positive emotions, life satisfaction and alignment with deeper values and purpose. While success reflects what we achieve, happiness reflects how we feel about our lives and ourselves. The two often overlap when goals are authentic and values-aligned, but they can also diverge, explaining why many achievers appear outwardly successful yet inwardly dissatisfied. This paradox is the entry point for the Seven Thieves explored in the chapters that follow.

How this book came about

As any business owner will tell you, we can all get lost working in our businesses every day rather than on them to ensure they deliver what we want them to. After completing my two-year term as President and Chair of the Board of the Career Development Institute in December 2023, I recognised the need to step back and reassess my business direction. To do this, I joined a programme with LinkedIn marketing expert Shelley Hutchinson, whose holistic, values-led approach resonated with me.

One of the first activities was to define our client avatars or buyer personas – fictional profiles of ideal clients. As a former marketeer, I understood the concept, but like many career development professionals, I found it uncomfortable. Choosing a single type of client felt inauthentic, as if I were excluding others I could help. Instead of asking us simply to create an avatar, Shelley posed a different question: *"Who do you most enjoy working with?"* That question led to a lightbulb moment and unlocked a deeper sense of purpose and enquiry.

At the time Shelley asked the question, I had just finished one of a series of coaching calls with a restless, bright and driven high achiever – let's call him Ivan. Ivan was increasingly frustrated by a series of false career dawns to which he had given his all, only to be left depleted each time. Our conversations were fast-moving and intense, with deliberate pauses as he grappled with difficult questions. Progress came in each session, and I often ended the calls smiling. In one particular conversation, we revisited themes from an earlier session that helped him realise the core issue – he was repeatedly trying to act like someone he was not in order to fit into traditional employment. It did not suit him or his emerging identity as an entrepreneur. I understood his drive to achieve intuitively because I recognised my own story, and my own cycles of depletion, in his struggles. You can read Ivan's full story in Chapter 5.

Reflecting on Shelley's question in light of that call made it clear to me who I most enjoy working with. More importantly, it provided a new lens through which to examine the many client stories I had encountered over the years and, in turn, to make sense of my own.

Anyone reading my career biography would be hard-pressed to describe me as anything other than a high achiever. While my biography reflects a relentless pursuit of conventional success, it does not reveal the cost of that striving – repeated cycles of burnout. It was the combination of my personal experiences and the familiar echoes I heard in the stories of my clients that sowed the seeds of curiosity leading to this book.

Through reflection, I began to see recurring patterns in the challenges achievers face. I tested these ideas in conversations with clients at different ages and stages, and through my *"Change Your Story"* LinkedIn newsletter and posts. The responses confirmed an undeniable pattern of themes that I came to call the Seven Thieves – forces that, alone or together, can steal joy and fulfilment from even the most capable achievers. Perhaps most worryingly of all, they steal unmeasurable amounts of human potential which should concern us all.

The achievement trap

I came to think of this pattern of themes as the achievement trap – the cycle in which the pursuit of success, if misdirected or unsustainable, undermines the very happiness it is meant to deliver. My aim in developing this model was not only to support those already struggling with the trap, but also to help prevent achievers from falling into it in the first place. Where support resources are stretched, it is often assumed that achievers can take care of themselves, but this is simply not the case as the stories in this book illustrate.

It is important to note that while this book focuses on people with an achiever orientation, the Seven Thieves are not unique forces that only apply to them. Anyone can experience their effects individually or in combination, though achievers are particularly vulnerable because of their need to drive and strive. It is this that turns the Seven Thieves into an almost inevitable process. It is also important to recognise that the thieves are not wholly negative. Some aspects, such as the pursuit of high standards, can have positive outcomes – we all want the software in aeroplanes to be perfect, for example. The danger arises when these tendencies become excessive, rigid or disconnected from authentic values.

Defining achievers

As David McClelland's Need for Achievement theory shows, achievers are individuals who orient their lives around goals and accomplishment. They are motivated not only by outcomes but by the striving itself – setting challenges, persisting through obstacles and deriving identity and meaning from what they accomplish. This orientation cuts across backgrounds, education levels and professional fields.

Commonplace in knowledge-based and professional contexts, achievers are found in business, law, medicine, technology, academia and other areas where career progression is tied to performance and recognition. Many have followed graduate and postgraduate routes into these roles. Yet achievement is by no means limited to the graduate pathway. Non-graduates often achieve distinction through entrepreneurship, the trades, vocational excellence and community leadership. Elite athletes, dancers, musicians and performers all demonstrate the same relentless pursuit of mastery and fulfilment, while others excel in public service, activism or creative industries. What unites these diverse groups is their orientation towards high standards, persistence and contribution.

Within this broad category, we can distinguish the following types of achievers:

- **Achievers** are individuals motivated by challenge, progress and accomplishment, balancing intrinsic and extrinsic goals as part of their growth.
- **High achievers** consistently surpass expectations in their chosen domains. They tend to combine intrinsic motivation (mastery, purpose, growth) with extrinsic drivers (recognition, advancement, rewards). High achievers are often resilient and capable of sustaining performance over time.
- **Overachievers** are those whose striving becomes excessive or misaligned. They often set unrealistically high standards, tie their self-worth to performance and struggle to feel satisfied even when successful. Overachievement is not about producing more than expected, but about striving in ways that undermine balance, authenticity and long-term wellbeing. In short, the difference lies less in how much they achieve, and more in how they go about achieving it. For example, a high achiever might work intensively on important projects while maintaining boundaries and relationships, whereas an overachiever might work compulsively on everything, sacrificing sleep, health and connections in pursuit of impossible standards. This drive sometimes reflects underlying insecurities or a need to manage emotional discomfort through external validation – patterns that may benefit from therapeutic support alongside career development work.
- **Underachievers** possess the talent, ability or potential to achieve highly but fall short of expectations. This may be due to low motivation, lack of opportunity, poor fit between strengths and environment or barriers such as disadvantage, discrimination or mental health challenges. In some cases, underachievement reflects hidden perfectionism which causes them to avoid effort to protect against failure or disconnection from authentic values and goals. While potentially a more complex client to help, with the proper support, underachievers may flourish into high achievers once barriers are addressed.

As always, it is important for us as practitioners to recognise which achiever pattern a client displays and to know when patterns may indicate underlying issues requiring specialist referral.

Ultimately, what binds these groups is not the field in which they operate but their relationship with striving and accomplishment. When balanced and values-aligned, achievement can be deeply fulfilling. When distorted or excessive, it leaves individuals vulnerable to the Seven Thieves explored in this book.

So, why do achievers matter anyway?

The cumulative loss of achiever talent is immense, both for the individuals themselves and for the wider economy and society. Much of it is entirely avoidable. When achievers burn out, disengage or exit prematurely, organisations lose not only highly capable people but also the innovation, leadership and productivity that others depend upon.

Recent evidence makes the scale of the problem clear. Gallup's *State of the Global Workplace 2025* report shows that the UK has one of the lowest engagement rates in Europe, with only 10% of employees engaged, compared to a global average of 21%. Just 46% of UK employees report "thriving" in life, and nearly one in three are actively seeking a new job. Daily stress, sadness and loneliness remain widespread, with 17% of UK employees reporting loneliness every day. Gallup calculates that if workplaces worldwide were fully engaged, an additional $9.6 trillion in productivity could be unlocked – equivalent to 9% of global GDP. We will return to this report again in Chapter 6.

In the UK, the Centre for Mental Health estimates the hidden productivity loss from presenteeism at over £100 billion annually, with employees losing up to 44 days of productivity per year in addition to sick leave. They also place the wider economic and social costs of mental ill health at up to £300 billion annually. According to the Mental Health Foundation, poor mental health costs UK employers £42–45 billion each year through presenteeism, sickness absence and staff turnover. According to the ONS (Office for National Statistics), sickness absence in 2024 reached 148.9 million days, the highest since records began, with each worker taking an average of 4.4 days, and mental health conditions accounting for almost one in ten cases.

Add to this the direct costs of avoidable grievances which often lead to redundancies, and the replacement of senior and professional staff, and the organisational impact becomes stark. The Chartered Institute of Personnel and Development (CIPD) estimates in its *Resourcing and Talent Planning survey* that replacing a senior professional can cost £30,000 or more once recruitment, onboarding and lost productivity are factored in. Beyond the numbers, the personal cost to individuals includes lost confidence, fractured identities, economic impact, strained relationships and prolonged recovery journeys.

This loss of talent does not begin in the workplace. It is visible much earlier in schools and universities, where a significant proportion of high-potential students underachieve relative to their abilities. According to researchers, Reis and McCoach, up to one in five gifted pupils fail to meet expectations, often due to perfectionism, disengagement or poor wellbeing. The regulator for the HE sector in England, the Office for Students, estimates that around one in four students report a mental health condition each year, with stress and perfectionism among the key contributors. These echo similar findings elsewhere in the other home nations. As a result, many leave education prematurely or struggle to transition effectively into work, representing a profound loss of both personal potential and societal investment.

As the CDI's Valuing Careers report says, *"careers are hugely important to people's wider life satisfaction and optimism indicators."* Supporting achievers to thrive so their potential is maximised enables them to develop sustainable careers for the benefit of themselves, their loved ones, the economy and society at large.

How to use this book

Supporting Achievers equips career development, careers education and HR professionals with the tools and strategies to identify, coach and support achievers of all ages and stages effectively. By fostering deeper self-awareness, career alignment and sustainable success, it enables achiever-profile clients to excel in ways that enhance their wellbeing, purpose and long-term career satisfaction.

The Seven Thieves introduced in *Supporting Achievers* can operate independently for some but typically work together as a progressive sequence for achievers, representing three stages of a journey from perfectionism through self-neglect to burnout.

Chapters 1–3 explore the core psychological drivers that make achievers, in particular, vulnerable to self-defeating patterns.

Chapters 4–5 examine the critical tipping points where strengths and drive start to become counterproductive.

Chapters 6–7 address the final stages of breakdown and the essential steps towards recovery and renewal.

Each chapter follows the same structure to ensure consistency and depth:

- **A true, anonymised client story** anchors the theory in lived experience.
- **Definition and framing:** The thief is defined and explored, including how it maps to personality traits using the Big Five/OCEAN framework.
- **Impact analysis:** The thief is examined across the following domains: workplace, education, age and career stage, gender, neurodivergence, socio-economic status (SES), culture and ethnicity, entrepreneurship, industry sectors and career lifespans.
- **Neuroscience insights:** Each chapter includes a concise section explaining the neurological responses associated with the thief, giving practitioners language they can use with clients.
- **Theory integration:** The client's story is analysed through five key theories. Rather than presenting these sequentially, the analysis is structured around the client's own words, reducing repetition and keeping the discussion grounded in lived experience. For those who wish to explore the models in more depth, a downloadable Theories Extra companion resource available on the Trotman website presents each theory individually with fuller explanation and analysis. To access, use the QR code or visit the web address at the start of this book.
- **Practical strategies and activities:** Every chapter concludes with coaching tools and reflective exercises. These draw from evidence-based approaches including Steven C. Hayes's Acceptance and Commitment Therapy (ACT), Spencer Niles, Norman Amundson and Hyung Joon Yoon's Hope Action Theory (HAT), Kristin

Neff's pioneering research on self-compassion, Jon Kabat-Zinn's Mindfulness-Based Stress Reduction (MBSR) and reflective practices such as journalling.

This consistent structure means you can read the book cover to cover or dip into specific chapters depending on client need. The aim is to provide you with both the conceptual understanding and the practical strategies to support achievers in unlocking sustainable success.

The final chapter offers a call to action, outlining strategic ideas for career development, careers education, executive coaching and HR professionals to ensure achievers are identified and receive the support they need.

Introducing the Seven Career Thieves

The Seven Career Thieves are evidence-based patterns observed first hand in my work supporting achievers of different career stages and ages. Each Career Thief can operate on its own, but more often they interact and build on one another, creating a cycle that steals potential, happiness, success, wellbeing and long-term career sustainability:

- **Perfectionism – the pursuit of impossible standards**
  Setting impossibly high benchmarks and struggling to feel satisfied, leaving little room for self-compassion.
- **Comparison – the trap of measuring up**
  Constantly judging progress against others, fuelling insecurity and eroding confidence.
- **Approval-Seeking – acting to please others**
  Relying on external validation at the expense of authentic direction and self-worth.
- **Overwhelm – where demand consistently exceeds capacity**
  Becoming overloaded as workload, responsibilities and expectations outpace capacity.
- **Depletion – when the energy tanks are empty**
  The gradual draining of energy and resilience through unrelenting striving and lack of recovery.
- **Disconnection – when connection and purpose are lost**
  Feeling cut off from values, meaning and belonging, leaving work and life unanchored.
- **Burnout – self-neglect through constantly prioritising work over wellbeing**
  The culmination of all the thieves, where health, identity and motivation collapse, often forcing a reckoning and the need for potential renewal.

In the chapters that follow, you will see how each of the Seven Thieves operates, and how, with the right insight and support, they can be challenged and overcome to reclaim fulfilment, resilience and sustainable success.

1 | The Thief of Perfectionism

The pursuit of impossible standards

> "Perfectionism is not a quest for the best.
> It is a pursuit of the worst in ourselves, the part that tells us
> that nothing we do will ever be good enough."
>
> Julia Cameron, American author, journalist and creator.

Geraldine's story

It was late autumn when I first met Geraldine, a second-year International Politics student, when she arrived at the Careers Service for an appointment. Established in 1919, Aberystwyth University's Department for International Politics is the oldest department of its kind in the world. It has a world-class reputation for its pioneering research and a long list of famous ministers, diplomats, civil servants and journalists among its alumni. Competition for places in undergraduate and postgraduate courses is usually fierce.

A bright, friendly and articulate student, Geraldine had a beautiful Northern Irish lilt, which she quickly used to describe the help she needed. She was struggling with exam nerves and had been sent my way by colleagues for help. We took a quick look at her academic record together, which confirmed that she had received straight A grades at A level and was on track for a first-class honours arts degree in international relations. With only one or two students gaining a first every year, I recognised that the stakes were high from Geraldine's perspective.

To help her settle into the conversation so she could recognise and reconnect with her obviously effective revision skills, we went through her strategy and processes, which were substantial. It soon became apparent that while she was confident in her preparation, the closer she came to completing her studies, the more she worried about her ability to perform well. She shared with me that her nerves had been getting progressively worse with every set of exams to the point that she was heading towards the early stages of having panic attacks and had required assistance in a recent exam. As she talked, her levels of anxiety were apparent.

We spent the rest of the session helping her understand what was happening to her and exploring her underlying fears and beliefs about taking exams. Geraldine spoke about feeling the weight on her shoulders as the first in her family to attend university and the weight of cultural expectations within her Catholic upbringing.

To help her develop tools to regain and regulate her emotions, I taught her a grounded breathing technique, to which she immediately responded well. She also learnt some visualisation techniques to help her reconnect with previous successful moments so that she was in a positive and effective state as she went into the exam room, reducing the impact of her nerves. Both interventions were designed to help her feel fully in control and present in the exam hall. Unsurprisingly, as I suspected she would, Geraldine mastered these so quickly and effectively that by the end of the session, I was confident she had enough tools to do well when the time came.

In early February of the following year, I noticed Geraldine's name on my schedule. She had booked a further appointment with me to discuss graduate job applications. I was eager to see her again, not least because I was keen to hear how the exams had gone.

I went out to collect her from the waiting area, using the short walk back to my office to gauge how she was. Her head was down, her shoulders sagged, her previously lively lilt was flat, and she was very agitated.

As we entered my office, I asked her how the exams had gone. "Terrible!" she replied. Her answer threw me off balance for a moment, as I had been convinced that the work we had done had given her the tools she needed.

I paused, took a breath and asked her, "What happened? What did you get?"

She slumped in her chair and said, "I got 99%."

For a moment, I thought I must have misheard and asked her to repeat herself. The same answer came back: "99%."

"99%?" I echoed. "What's wrong with that?"

Tears welled up as she replied, "My father asked what happened to the other 1%."

Although extreme, Geraldine's experience and reaction exemplify perfectionism and what happens when success becomes the lens through which individuals measure their entire self-worth.

*****

So, what is perfectionism?

The American Psychological Association defines perfectionism as *"the tendency to demand of others or of oneself an extremely high or even flawless level of performance, in excess of what is required by the situation. It is associated with depression, anxiety, eating disorders, and other mental health problems."*

From a personality trait perspective, perfectionism is one of Raymond Cattell's 16 Personality Factors, who defined it as *"the pressing need to uphold high standards in work, relationships, and life in general – with every detail under control."*

Perfectionism is now widely recognised as a complex, multidimensional construct. Evolutionary psychologists believe that perfectionism has evolved as a way to signal competence and reliability to potential allies and mates for reproduction, help to secure and maintain social rank within hierarchical groups, reduce the risk of social exclusion (historically a threat to survival), and demonstrate commitment to group standards and values.

While the different main theories explore perfectionism from different perspectives, ranging from personality traits, self-concept and interpersonal expectations to cognitive processes, overall researchers argue it is both a personality trait and an adaptive social strategy with the following common themes:

- the pursuit of high standards,
- the merging of self-worth with success, and
- the emotional cost of falling short.

Most models now also acknowledge that perfectionism exists on a spectrum centred around two forms. It can be adaptive and foster growth in some, while for others it can be maladaptive, which creates emotional strain. This emphasises the value of context and self-awareness. Let's look at the difference between the two forms:

Adaptive behaviour and traits (constructive) in an achiever can be inspiring when there is self-congruence. This constructive approach enables individuals to cope effectively with their environment and achieve positively without much self-criticism. When perfectionism is more about goals than fear, it can lead to positive outcomes which boost life satisfaction.

From a trait perspective, the Big Five OCEAN model of personality **(Openness, Conscientiousness, Extraversion, Agreeableness** and **Neuroticism)** associates more adaptive traits with those with a higher tendency towards Conscientiousness. Adaptive perfectionism is linked to motivation and achievement – often an important feature of academic success.

Maladaptive behaviour and traits (known as dysfunctional) tend to be more damaging and hinder an individual's ability to cope, adjust or function effectively, often resulting in negative consequences and a prolonged sense of striving without success. This behaviour is motivated by fear or strict self-standards. It is destructive in nature and can cause individuals to indulge in excessive planning, rumination, procrastination, anxiety and stress, which paradoxically can significantly reduce productivity and wellbeing. Frequently used as a coping mechanism, it is also characterised by overthinking, worrying about failure and harsh self-judgement as the individual seeks to be flawless and avoid criticism and rejection. When we equate achievement with personal value, even small failures can trigger disproportionate self-criticism.

Again, from a trait perspective, the OCEAN test associates those with higher **Neuroticism** with being more likely to show maladaptive traits. This has implications for wellbeing, as experts have identified that older adults with high perfectionism and Neuroticism have a higher mortality risk.

Perfectionism is often rooted in external validation. In this context, it is not about striving for excellence but rather about striving to feel safe, seen and secure through earning acceptance and approval.

While some perfectionists may start with internal goals, over time, their self-evaluation becomes entangled with how others perceive them. This can lead to chronic stress, fear of failure and difficulty experiencing genuine satisfaction or self-worth. Some perfectionists are driven by the belief that only extraordinary achievement earns attention, love or purpose. To be "just average" feels like erasure. External validation becomes the proof that they matter.

Perfectionism provides a shield against perceived abandonment by loved ones, peers, employers or society. A deep-seated worry about not being good enough and making mistakes or falling short can create a fear of shame, which ironically can be offset by gaining external validation. Adopting a perfectionist approach addresses a fear of losing control in a chaotic or uncertain world by creating emotional safety. Those who have been raised in environments where high expectations and conditional affection are the norm often internalise the idea that their value is tied to making others proud, so they do all in their power to avoid letting people down and disappointing them.

Why should we be worried about perfectionism?

We live in an achievement culture that masks an increasingly virulent underlying existential vulnerability, as Geraldine's fragility demonstrates. Perfectionism is rising and has become a significant issue in both workplaces and education alike.

In the **workplace**, recent research conducted by the Hardin Group in partnership with the Social Research Lab at the University of Northern Colorado found that 92% of employees report perfectionist tendencies, and 66% of organisations see it as a significant concern. Perfectionism is known to lead to procrastination, which adversely affects productivity. It can also contribute to poor relationships and burnout, which we will explore in later chapters. Another recent study by Emily Kleszewski et al. has shown that perfectionistic concerns impede the achievement of work objectives, which in turn reinforces perfectionistic concerns. Perfectionism is closely linked to anxiety, depression and physical health issues such as fatigue, cardiovascular strain and early mortality.

In **education**, perfectionism has risen sharply, particularly among university students. In the UK, research shows 66% of students like

4

Geraldine identify as perfectionists, and student support services report a sevenfold increase in cases of burnout and distress. Academic perfectionism affects performance and mental health, contributing to dropout, depression and suicidal thoughts.

First-generation students are also more likely to develop perfectionism. This is due to heightened familial and societal expectations, as we saw with Geraldine. While striving for excellence can drive academic achievement, the maladaptive forms of perfectionism are closely linked with adverse mental health outcomes, imposter syndrome and chronic stress, as in Geraldine's case.

When it comes to **gender**, Geraldine comes off worse, too. Women tend to experience more socially prescribed and self-critical perfectionism, which contributes to imposter syndrome, overwork and career hesitation. Men are more likely to apply for opportunities early, while women wait until they meet all the criteria. Sadly, these patterns are reinforced by systemic bias, early gender norms and unequal task delegation.

Neurodivergent individuals, such as those with ADHD or autism, often show perfectionism in their high-quality work but may often pay the price through inefficient working and stress. Whether an individual is neurodivergent or living with other disabilities, they frequently feel pressure to overperform to counter societal stigma. They often internalise failure, leading to fatigue, low self-esteem and poor health.

Socio-economic status (SES) also influences whether individuals develop perfectionist tendencies. In affluent communities, perfectionism is often linked to external validation and conditional approval. Adolescents, particularly girls, are prone to internalising expectations around academic, financial and personal success, leading to anxiety, avoidance and burnout.

Finally, from a national perspective, **collectivist cultures** like those in Asia often strongly emphasise social harmony, duty and meeting family or societal expectations. This culture can cause individuals to feel intense pressure to meet external standards to maintain group belonging and avoid shame. In more individualistic cultures such as the UK and US, where autonomy, personal achievement and self-actualisation are prized culturally, individuals like Geraldine often perceive high standards as a reflection of their worth and identity.

Perfectionism and sectors

While perfectionism exists in all sectors, some consistently report high levels of perfectionism. Typically, these are:

- **Healthcare, law and STEM**, which demand precision and carry high stakes, thereby reinforcing both adaptive and maladaptive tendencies.
- **Creative fields**, such as design and tailoring, where artistry is blended with scrutiny, also often fuel an individual's perfectionistic drive.

- **Academia and professional services** where perfectionism is often rewarded, but often at the cost of wellbeing.
- **Entrepreneurs** are especially vulnerable. Though perfectionism drives ambition, it can inhibit innovation and delay progress.

Perfectionism across the career lifespan

When we look at different ages and stages of an individual's career journey, maladaptive perfectionism causes a range of challenges at each stage:

Early careers: While adaptive perfectionism enhances confidence and decision-making, maladaptive perfectionism leads to stress and hesitation. High-achieving students and under-represented STEM groups are especially at risk of this and need support to thrive.

Mid-careers: Again, while adaptive perfectionism supports resilience, maladaptive tendencies tend to block growth, leaving potential untapped. Individuals who work for a boss or in a culture where flawlessness is valued over learning often experience enhanced anxiety and low self-worth. This frequently leads to an exit by choice or due to grievance.

Late careers and retirement: Perfectionism presents a significant challenge when it comes to retirement. Without career structures in place, individuals may experience identity loss, increased self-criticism and isolation. Acceptance, redefined self-worth and support can help transform this life stage into one of meaning and fulfilment.

The neuroscience of perfectionism

In terms of the brain, perfectionism is more than a mindset; it is wired in. Neuroscientists have identified brain mechanisms associated with different perfectionist tendencies, distinguishing between more adaptive and maladaptive patterns.

The **anterior cingulate cortex** (ACC) plays a central role in performance monitoring, error detection and conflict resolution. In adaptive perfectionism, heightened ACC activity helps individuals detect errors and adjust their behaviour, for example, by slowing down after a mistake to correct it. The ACC also supports fundamental cognitive functions such as motivation, decision-making, learning and cost-benefit analysis.

Research shows that individuals with maladaptive perfectionist concerns, especially those characterised by worry over mistakes and doubts about actions, often exhibit increased grey matter volume in the ACC, a pattern linked to higher levels of anxiety and depression.

In addition, these individuals may show reduced activation in the **prefrontal cortex** (PFC) when performing tasks that require error tolerance. The **amygdala**, the brain's "smoke detector" for emotional and survival threats, often displays hyperreactivity in response to perceived failure. When connectivity between the amygdala and the PFC is poor, emotional regulation is impaired, making it more challenging to manage negative self-evaluation and perpetuating cycles of self-criticism.

The brain's reward circuitry, responsible for motivation, reinforcement and pleasure, also plays a crucial role in perfectionism. Two key components are the Ventral Tegmental Area (VTA) and the Nucleus Accumbens (NAcc).

Located in the midbrain, the VTA produces dopamine, a neurotransmitter linked to reward and motivation. When someone achieves a goal, particularly one tied to high personal standards or external approval, the VTA releases dopamine. This is sent to the NAcc, which acts as a bridge between motivation and action, interpreting the dopamine signal as pleasure or relief.

In perfectionists, this reward pathway may reinforce the belief that achievement is the only route to self-worth or emotional safety. The relief that follows success is often less about satisfaction and more about avoiding criticism or feelings of failure. Over time, this can create a self-reinforcing neural loop, where success leads to dopamine release, which provides temporary relief, reinforcing the need to repeat the cycle. While this can drive high performance, it also contributes to chronic stress, burnout and fragile self-esteem, especially when perfection is perceived as the only acceptable standard.

This neurobiological loop helps explain why perfectionism is so persistent and highlights its addictive nature. Breaking free often requires shifting towards intrinsic motivation based on personal meaning, curiosity or growth, rather than for external validation or avoidance of failure.

From a gender perspective, there are differences which have been identified through brain imaging. Women are likely to show greater activity in areas associated with emotional and social processing and are more self-referential in their thinking. Their thoughts and self-concept are more likely to be relational and interpersonally focused, whereas men are more likely to be individually or task-focused. Women tend more towards using emotion-focused coping strategies and are also significantly more likely than men to dwell on problems and emotions ("ruminative coping"), whereas men are more likely to seek a problem-focused strategy. These differences explain why women tend to suffer from higher rates of anxiety and depression than men. It is also worth noting how race, culture and disability can intersect with gender cumulatively to amplify these patterns further.

Perfectionism theory in action

Understanding Geraldine's experience through theory highlights how perfectionism often hides beneath achievement and creates deep emotional costs. By anchoring the analysis around her own words, we can see how different theories intersect to explain her distress and suggest practical ways forward.

"Terrible - I only got 99%"

This phrase epitomises maladaptive perfectionism: extraordinary achievement framed as failure.

- **Higgins' Self-Discrepancy Theory** explains Geraldine's collapse as the clash between her actual self (99%), her ideal self (flawless success) and her ought-self (her father's expectations). The discrepancy fuels anxiety and self-doubt.
- **Frost's Multidimensional Model** reveals multiple strands at play: concern over mistakes, parental expectations, parental criticism and doubts about action. Her academic organisation was strong, but her beliefs made success feel fragile.
- **Hewitt and Flett's Multidimensional Scale** helps explain why the comment hurt so deeply: Geraldine combined self-oriented striving with socially prescribed perfectionism – believing others demanded flawlessness and fearing rejection if she failed.
- **Shafran et al.'s Clinical Perfectionism Model** shows the cognitive loop: biased evaluation, achievement-dependent self-worth and negative self-talk. Success was never enough, so distress followed automatically.

"My father asked what happened to the other 1%"

This comment crystallises how perfectionism becomes internalised through family and culture.

- **Parental expectations and criticism** (Frost) provide a direct lens: external judgement was absorbed as self-criticism.
- **Socially prescribed perfectionism** (Hewitt and Flett) explains how external pressure translated into internal strain – with conditional approval shaping her identity.
- **Stoeber and Otto's distinction between perfectionist strivings and perfectionist concerns** shows Geraldine's perfectionist concerns (fear of mistakes, doubts, worry about criticism) outweighed her strivings, tipping her profile into maladaptive territory.
- **Gaudreau and Thompson's 2 × 2 Model** suggests she sat in "mixed perfectionism": high standards coupled with evaluative concerns, producing both high performance and high anxiety.

"If I'm not perfect, I'll let people down"

Geraldine's underlying fear of disappointing her father reflects the emotional cost of perfectionism and indicates potential unhelpful beliefs.

- **Self-Discrepancy Theory** highlights how ought-self obligations generate guilt and unease.

- **Perfectionism** frames this as overdependence on achievement for self-worth.
- **ACT (Acceptance and Commitment Theory – explored later in this chapter)** provides an antidote: recognising thoughts as mental events, not truths, and re-orienting towards chosen values rather than impossible standards.

The influence of background

Geraldine's background amplified her perfectionism.

- As a **first-generation student**, success carried the burden of family pride.
- From a **Catholic upbringing**, conditional approval and fear of guilt reinforced strict self-evaluation.
- The **evolutionary perspective** reminds us that perfectionism can function as a strategy to maintain social rank and belonging, but in modern academic contexts, this can become maladaptive and harmful.

What Geraldine's story shows us

Geraldine's case illustrates the multi-layered dynamics of perfectionism. *"I only got 99%"* captures the biased self-evaluation central to clinical perfectionism and self-discrepancy theory. *"My father asked what happened to the other 1%"* shows how parental expectations and socially prescribed standards reinforce perfectionist concerns, tipping achievement into distress. Her unspoken belief, *"If I'm not perfect, I'll let people down,"* reveals the deep emotional dependency of self-worth on external validation.

Together, these words demonstrate how perfectionism is not simply about high standards but about identity, belonging and emotional safety.

The theories converge on three insights:

- **Perfectionism merges self-worth with achievement**, making success fragile and failure catastrophic.
- **External pressures intensify internalised standards**, with family, culture and context amplifying risk.
- **Recovery requires reframing, values alignment and flexible coping**, helping clients shift from fear-driven perfection to excellence, self-compassion and sustainable motivation.

In the next section, we will explore how coaching using the ABCDE model and ACT principles helped Geraldine challenge perfectionist beliefs, separate her worth from achievement and embrace excellence over impossible standards

Decoding and resolving Geraldine's perfectionist mindset

To counteract the negative impact of Geraldine's conversation with her father, I encouraged her to take an objective look at her results from a fact-based perspective. We talked about what mark denoted the threshold for a first-class honours grade. She indicated that she knew that it was 70%. I then asked her to remind me what mark she achieved, and she reiterated her grade mark of 99%.

My final questions and responses were designed to help her reframe her mark and related beliefs about her ability and talent through the lens of excellence rather than perfectionism. I asked her about the worldwide reputation the department had, how competitive it was to get in, and if she could name any of the many famous and successful alumni at the top of their game who had also studied there. Finally, I asked her what the likelihood is of getting a perfect 100% in an arts degree in a world-class department.

Her face changed, and a smile appeared briefly before she started laughing as she realised how well she had done so far. I reassured her that parents usually only want the best for their children so they can be happy, healthy and financially independent. I never saw Geraldine again, but knew that she had understood that excellence was good enough, a realisation which I hoped would serve her for life.

*****

Decoding what clients are thinking

As practitioners, our role is often to join the dots to help us enable the client to understand what is going on for them. As we saw in Geraldine's case, her emotions, challenges to her sense of self and a sense of social comparison were all being tested and were relatively easy to identify.

Sometimes it is not so obvious, and this is where cognitive-based psychotherapist Albert Ellis's ABCDE model provides an effective approach to detect and reveal a client's unhelpful strategies and thinking so we can work together to create change. The model is based on the premise that the things we believe and the stories we tell ourselves shape the way we respond to challenging events. When we change our beliefs, we can replace old response patterns with better ones.

The model consists of the following five steps:

1. **A**ctivating event
2. **B**eliefs
3. **C**onsequences
4. **D**ispute
5. **E**ffect

Using the ABCDE model to help Geraldine move forward

Activating event

As we know, Geraldine was triggered by her father's comments about her exam result. Letting her tell her story provided the clues both verbally and non-verbally, leading to insights into what she was challenged by and how she felt.

By listening and watching carefully, I was able to hear and see where there were cognitive bias, cognitive dissonance and cognitive distortion at play.

Cognitive biases are inherent tendencies in our thinking which cause us to favour information that backs up what we already believe and ignore evidence that goes against what we think. These biases stem from the way we naturally think, process information and make choices. People often think of them as mental shortcuts or heuristics that help us decide what to do quickly, but can also get us wrong.

Some examples are:

- *Confirmation bias*, where we favour information that confirms existing beliefs while ignoring contradictory evidence,

- *Being Available Heuristic*, where we put too much stock in events that are easy to remember, even if they don't happen very often, and

- *Anchoring bias* is when we rely too much on the first piece of information we see, even if it is not important.

According to Buster Benson, the reason we use cognitive biases is to solve one of four problems: information overload, a lack of meaning, the need to act fast and figuring out what needs to be remembered for later. To make working with biases easier, Benson has developed a comprehensive cognitive bias codex in the form of a handy wheel we can use for our own development and with clients to help them understand how bias informs their thinking. Once the bias(es) at play have been identified, we can then gently challenge or reframe something with a client as needed.

Cognitive dissonance is different. The term describes the psychological discomfort felt when a person's actions conflict with their beliefs or values. First proposed by psychologist Leon Festinger in 1957, the theory suggests people are motivated to reduce this tension by changing their behaviour, adjusting their beliefs or rationalising the inconsistency. This gives the individual a sense of internal psychological consistency.

Cognitive dissonance is often seen in healthcare settings, for instance, where someone wants to give up smoking because they know it will bring them health benefits, but continues not to do so. Sometimes, however, when the conflict is below the surface, clients need help to resolve what is often a values-related conflict so they can move forward. This is frequently the case in careers work.

The second way our thinking affects us is through **cognitive distortion,** as evident in Geraldine's case. Cognitive distortions are more specific, distorted and often illogical ways of thinking that create negative feelings and behaviour in an individual.

Some examples are:

- *All-or-nothing thinking* where everything is black and white,

- *Overgeneralisation* when we jump to big, negative conclusions from a single bad event,

- *Catastrophising* when we imagine the worst that could happen, and

- *Emotional reasoning*, the idea that feelings show what's really going on.

In general, cognitive distortions are less common but more challenging and dangerous than cognitive biases. Biases are less dangerous and more common than cognitive distortions, and have been linked to depression and increased levels of worry and anxiety.

Some of the fear-based tell-tale phrases and underlying fears and needs to watch for are:

- *"If I'm not perfect, people won't want me."* (Fear of rejection)

- *"If I fail, it proves I'm not good enough."* (Fear of shame)

- *"If I do everything right, nothing bad will happen."* (Need for control)

- *"If I don't stand out, I'll disappear."* (Fear of being ordinary or not standing out)

- *"If I'm not perfect, I'll let people down."* (Fear of disappointing people)

As well as exploring thinking through questioning, we can use what Damasio called **somatic markers.** These "denote how we code experiences as either positive (guiding stars) and negative (black holes)." Here, emotion gives us data and insights which provide coaching fuel for us to use through reflecting what we see back as the lead into asking well-formed questions that help to explore the cognitive landscape.

Geraldine's story illustrates all elements outlined above, creating a window of opportunity to help her move forward more comfortably.

Beliefs

When we have those verbal and non-verbal insights into a client's world, we can start exploring what underpins their reaction. It was clear that Geraldine had always been expected to achieve top marks. While some of this was internally motivated, some of this was clearly driven by her father's expectations. From her reactions to my questions and her own comments, it was clear that Geraldine believed that she had to be perfect to gain her father's approval. Underpinning this was a further belief that she had to be perfect to be good enough.

Consequences

The pressures of her beliefs were increasingly causing her to feel highly anxious. While she could put in hours of revision using sound techniques, she could not control what would appear on the paper. This contributed to the pressure she was feeling internally.

Dispute

Exploring the reality of grade boundaries and her department's status gave her new data and insights which helped her to change her perspective on what was possible. Giving her a parental perspective also helped Geraldine to think about her father's expectations differently. She recognised that her father only wanted the best for her.

Effect

Once she realised the near impossibility of what she was striving to achieve and gained a different perspective, she was able to consider and adopt a new belief centred on excellence rather than perfection.

Helping clients to ACT differently

As well as using ABCDE as a model that can be explained easily to and used with a client, I often use concepts from Acceptance and Commitment Theory (ACT) developed in the 1990s by Steve C. Hayes. In practical terms, ACT introduces metaphors, mindfulness and committed action, which can integrate well with journalling, identity work or coaching exercises. The approach uses behavioural analysis to create psychological flexibility and is proving increasingly beneficial in alleviating career anxiety and workplace stress. Where perfectionism tries to avoid discomfort through control, ACT invites us to make space for discomfort while still doing what matters. It does this by encouraging people to be more aware, to open up and do what matters so they can live the life they want and has six elements:

1. **Cognitive diffusion:** This means separating ourselves from our thoughts, whether true or not, by observing them as clouds that pass through our minds.
2. **Acceptance:** These unwanted thoughts and feelings can exist without us trying to control or avoid them.
3. **Present-moment awareness:** Encouragement to be present rather than ruminating over the past or worrying about the future.
4. **Self-as-context:** Here we develop more of a transcendent approach where we see ourselves as observers of our experiences rather than being defined by them.
5. **Values:** When we become clear about what truly matters to us,we can develop a deep and chosen life direction.
6. **Committed action:** This means using those values to help us take purposeful steps even if we face inner discomfort in doing so.

Hope Action Theory also contains some helpful concepts which I draw on with clients. Developed by Niles, Amundson and Yoon, it encourages a hopeful, goal-directed process. Hope combines agency (confidence to act) and pathways (ability to find routes forward). Hope Action Theory highlights six competencies: self-reflection, clarity, visioning, goal-setting, action and adaptation. Together these build resilience and purposeful career navigation.

Activities to create changes in perfectionism thinking and behaviour

As practitioners, we sometimes have to be brave and trust ourselves while holding a safe space for the client to explore issues which we may find uncomfortable at first. Doing so helps both us and the client grow. From a client wellbeing and safety perspective, we also need to remember to evaluate when the work we are intending to do is appropriate for this client or whether it would be better to advise or support a referral to a medically qualified practitioner, particularly if, rather than presenting purely with distress alone, the client seems depressed as well. If you are unsure which it is, encouraging or providing links for a referral to a suitably qualified medical professional/therapist is the most appropriate option. As an immediate support offering, sharing safe-to-use techniques like breathwork would also be both wise and appropriate (see Chapter 7 for more on this).

Here are three different activities you could use to help clients move forward effectively, which reflect the ethos behind both the ABCDE and ACT blended with other helpful approaches.

ACTIVITY 1: NOTICING AND CHANGING THOUGHTS THROUGH JOURNALLING

One of the key principles of ACT is that language and thought processes are seen as central contributors to psychological suffering. To reduce this, ACT encourages us to diffuse ourselves from recurring thoughts such as "I must be perfect."

It is hard to separate ourselves from our thoughts if they carry significant weight with them. While anecdotal evidence claims that we have up to 60,000 thoughts a day, in 2020, scientists from Queen's University developed a method using brain scanning to indirectly detect when one thought ends and another begins by identifying "thought worms." These are continuous patterns of brain activity linked to a single idea and mark transitions between distinct thoughts. As a result of their research, we now know that we have, on average, 6,200 thoughts a day.

Before any of us can disempower or change unhelpful thoughts which trigger unhelpful behaviours, we must first be aware of them. This is where journalling can be very helpful. It equips both us as practitioners and our clients with a tool to recognise patterns of thinking. Once we, and clients, have identified our individual patterns, we can then either smile in recognition as they pass like clouds in our thinking, or we can choose to change them (see later activities).

Journalling provides an excellent, simple and low-cost way to capture our thoughts and notice patterns of thinking over time by capturing personal thoughts, feelings and insights. As an approach, journalling is known to reduce anxiety, help with ruminating, create awareness, help to regulate emotions, improve memory, encourage an individual to open up and even speed up physical healing, as studies have shown.

While many clients have a strong sense of self-understanding and will not need much support to make sense of journal entries, we can help those who struggle with self-understanding more by using tools such as Plutchik's petal-shaped wheel of emotions, which reflects the various intensities of each of our primary emotions.

Sharing this tool with clients helps to explore, name and normalise the emotions they are feeling. It creates a deeper understanding of an individual's inner emotional landscape and can aid emotional regulation, communication and empathy.

As practitioners, once a client has named their strongest negative emotion, we help them identify the fear driving it. We can then flip the exercise to the positive: that is, help them to name the positive state they are aiming for and what would support it. Because the brain tends toward negativity, deliberately foregrounding positive emotions helps restore balance.

It never ceases to surprise me how much clients benefit from the act of acknowledging their fear, even before we start work together on helping them to be braver and gain a different perspective through reframing and other techniques such as journalling.

You can work with clients to set up a series of prompt-based journalling questions such as this sequence:

1. Today/this week, the main things which have challenged me have been...
    (Describe what happened and why it mattered.)
2. I responded to these challenges and events by...
    (Note your thoughts, actions or reactions – what helped, and what didn't?)
3. Looking back with the benefit of time and distance, I realise that...
    (What have you learnt about yourself, your thinking patterns or your needs?)
4. Next time, I'd like to respond differently by...
    (What small, supportive change could you make?)

This creates a structure you can go through with the client when you next work with them to help them to anchor learning and continue to develop with your support.

An alternative to creating prompt questions around topics is simply to ask a client to pay particular attention to anything related to a specific theme, such as happiness or success. The act of noticing, recording and exploring thoughts and feelings around topics such as this helps to surface hidden issues and challenges which practitioners can help clients to make sense of and change as necessary.

Journalling is also recommended by Associate Professor at the University of Texas, Kristin Neff, as a tool to use and build self-compassion. Neff describes self-compassion as a way of relating to the ever-changing experience of who we are with kindness and acceptance – especially when we fail or feel inadequate. This helps us to deal with the ups and downs of life. Self-compassion does not require feeling better than anyone else. It simply requires acknowledging the shared and imperfect human condition we all experience and treating ourselves with kindness rather than judgement, seeking connection rather than isolation and reconciling suffering in a mindful way so it can pass.

Neff's model of self-compassion includes six elements which fall into two groups:

- enhancing self-kindness, recognising common humanity and practising mindfulness, and
- reducing self-judgement, reducing feelings of isolation and overidentification with negative thoughts.

Neff encourages clients to use these as a lens for journalling and offers examples on her website.

Her research counters misconceptions of it being selfish or demotivating and instead shows the role self-compassion has to play in fostering a greater sense of wellbeing.

The latest research shows that one of the best things we can do for clients in difficult times is to help them to give themselves the same compassion as they would to others. Self-compassion involves offering oneself understanding and encouragement in times of distress, whether these stem from personal faults and shortcomings or challenges imposed by outside circumstances.

Many clients enjoy the benefits of learning to journal and continue to use it as an approach long after their career coaching interventions have come to an end.

ACTIVITY 2: FINDING FLOW TO INTERRUPT ANXIETY

According to the Mental Health Foundation, **anxiety** is a *"common emotional state characterised by feelings of unease, such as worry or fear, that can range from mild to severe."* A natural response to stress, it can motivate or protect us. However, if it becomes persistent or overwhelming, it can disrupt daily life and cause physical symptoms. While not always a disorder, chronic anxiety may require support, lifestyle changes or professional help to manage effectively. According to global health and care company Bupa, in the UK, 15% of people in employment have a mental health condition, and around 875,000 suffer from work-related stress, depression and anxiety. Anxiety often stems from thinking about the future as we imagine catastrophes waiting for us around the corner. It can also come from thinking about previous difficult events from the past. Helping clients to spend more time being present serves to interrupt their thought worms.

One way to negate the impact of our unhelpful thinking is to be in a state of what the American psychologist Mihaly Csikszentmihalyi termed *"flow."* He described it as *"a state of heightened focus and immersion in activities such as art, play and work."* That happens when, by following your passion and energy, work becomes play as you discover the joy of being lost in the moment.

As Csikszentmihalyi indicated, we need eight elements to experience flow:

- having clear goals every step of the way,
- having a balance between skills and level of challenge so it is not so easy you get bored, and not so challenging it tips you into anxiety,
- having immediate feedback to actions,
- concentrating so deeply on the task in hand that you are not aware of distractions,
- being completely involved in the present moment so that the activity becomes an end in itself,
- having a strong sense of control and being free from any worry about failing,

- experiencing an altered sense of time so that it either evaporates or the clock seems to stand still, and finally,
- having no sense of self and ego, so we are no longer self-conscious.

Helping clients to recognise when they are in flow and learn how to get into flow quickly gives them a way to become fully present. This is easy to do. Having explained the concept of flow to your client, simply ask them to remember a time when they were in flow, relive it in their mind's eye like a movie, and then notice what it feels like to be truly present rather than worrying about the past or anticipating a crisis in the future. Get them to spend a few moments noticing their breathing, how their body feels and how clear their mind is.

Once the client has identified one time when they were in flow, asking them to find further examples will enable them to work out what conditions they need to get into flow easily in the future. This will help them to reduce anxiety, increase positivity and become more positive through creating work of high quality.

Another great activity to ask your clients to consider doing in their private time is to experience the ancient Turkish art of Ebru or water marbling. Recognised by UNESCO, the practice focuses on dropping, sprinkling and brushing colour pigments onto a pan of oily water to create patterns which can then be transferred onto paper or silk.

The reason this works so well goes back to perfectionist clients wanting a high level of control as a way of preventing failure, one of the big underlying motivations associated with perfectionist profiles. Doing activities like Ebru causes the perfectionist client to cede control, as they cannot control the water and literally must go with the flow. This can lead to feelings of being free to play and experience without concerns about being judged. This is a powerful way to help clients experience other mindsets and ways of being before perfectionism took over.

ACTIVITY 3: BUILDING AN AUTHENTIC SELF, USING "I AM" IDENTITY BOARDS

As we all experience more of life, it is easy to become disconnected from our authentic selves. This third activity encourages clients to reconnect with their true selves and make values-led consciously aligned choices about who they want to become as individuals. The activity aids self-validation, increases agency and self-efficacy and can be done as a facilitated or independent activity.

Creating an "I am" board helps clients to develop greater authenticity by exploring, reframing and internalising their values and associated beliefs of self.

It uses the visualisation ethos of creating a vision board and encourages individuals to reflect on the positive personal qualities they already have and create a pathway to qualities they want to develop using an affirmations-style approach.

To do this activity, you/your client will need the same types of things as are needed to create a vision board: a large piece of paper or cardboard to use as a base for the board they are creating; old magazines; scissors; glue; and coloured pens (marker pens and highlighters work well). Your client may want to use a picture of themselves too if that is helpful for them to include it. I would suggest treading gently here, as some clients may not want to do this if they have negative values about their appearance.

If they are happy to use a photo of themselves, ask them to position it in the middle of the large sheet of paper or board and write the words "I am" underneath. If they prefer not to use their image, then they just need to write the phrase "I am" in the style of their choice.

Then get them to go through the old magazines and cut out adjectives which describe who they are now or how they want to be in the future.

Here are two questions to help them do so:

- "What words would you use to describe who you are now?"
- "What words would you like to use to describe how you want to feel and be in the future?"

Your role as a facilitator is to support and encourage exploration and choice while gently challenging negative values and unhelpful beliefs.

You may need to explain the difference between values and beliefs. I explain values as the principles, standards or qualities that are held in high regard across society. In contrast, beliefs are developed from real experiences in the past which we hold to be true in the present, but which may no longer be true and may not serve us.

As we identified earlier, perfectionism is contextual and a continuum, so reminding clients to consider themselves from the perspective of every area of their lives will help them to recognise and appreciate their overall qualities more.

Once your client has created their board, encouraging them to display it somewhere that they will see it every day will help to confirm and embed the new values of self. If they prefer not to display it, then taking a photograph they can see on their desktop, laptop or PC or in paper form that they can carry around with them or keep in their desk drawer will achieve the same outcome.

Summary

As you have read, perfectionism is a complex and multifaceted trait and behaviour construct. When we help clients to recognise perfectionism, its fears and root causes, they can learn how to recognise these tendencies in their everyday lives, make different choices and be kinder to themselves. The primary underlying fear of not being enough depends largely on checking to see how people measure up to others. Comparison is the second thief which steals our joy and happiness and is the theme of the next chapter.

1. The Thief of Perfectionism
At a glance

Definition: "The tendency to demand of others or of oneself an extremely high or even flawless level of performance, in excess of what is required by the situation. It is associated with depression, anxiety, eating disorders, and other mental health problems." (APA)

Key theories and models:

1. **Self-Discrepancy Theory (Higgins, 1987):** Gaps between actual self, ideal self and ought-self create emotional distress and perfectionist behaviours.
2. **Frost's 6-Dimension Model (1990):** Concern over mistakes, personal standards, parental expectations/criticism, doubting actions, organisation.
3. **Hewitt and Flett's 3-Dimension Model (1991):** Self-oriented, other-oriented and socially prescribed perfectionism affecting interpersonal relationships.

Impact and context:

66% of UK students identify as perfectionists; sevenfold increase in burnout cases.

Women experience more socially prescribed perfectionism; men have more task-focused perfectionism.

Prevalent in healthcare, law, STEM, creative fields, academia and professional services.

- **Early career:** Enhances confidence but increases stress.
- **Mid-career:** Blocks growth.
- **Late career:** Complicates retirement.

Warning signs:

- **Fear of rejection:** "If I'm not perfect, people won't want me."
- **Fear of shame:** "If I fail, it proves I'm not good enough."
- **Need for control:** "If I do everything right, nothing bad will happen."
- **Fear of being ordinary:** "If I don't stand out, I'll disappear."
- **Fear of disappointing others:** "If I'm not perfect, I'll let people down."
- **Fear of abandonment:** Avoiding perceived abandonment through achievement.
- **Conditional self-worth:** Value tied entirely to performance and success.

The pursuit of impossible standards

4. **Shafran, Cooper and Fairburn's Clinical Perfectionism Model (2002):** Self-evaluation is substantially affected by pursuing excessively high standards despite adverse consequences.
5. **Stoeber and Otto's Perfectionist Strivings versus Perfectionist Concerns (2006):** shows how high standards aid achievement while worry about mistakes fuels anxiety, depression and low self-esteem.
6. **2 × 2 Model (Gaudreau and Thompson):** Four types: Non-perfectionist, Pure Personal Standards Perfectionism (Pure PSP), Pure Evaluative Concerns Perfectionism (Pure ECP), Mixed perfectionism (high PSP and high ECP). .

Neuroscience:

Perfectionism is wired into the brain through specific neural pathways:

- **Anterior cingulate cortex:** Error detection and performance monitoring.
- **Prefrontal cortex:** Reduced activation in error tolerance.
- **Amygdala:** Hyperreactive to perceived failure.
- **Reward circuitry:** VTA and NAcc create addictive achievement loops.

Dopamine release from achievement creates self-reinforcing cycles where success provides temporary relief, reinforcing the need to repeat the pattern.

Key coaching activities:

1. **Journalling for Thought Awareness:** Uses structured prompts to identify perfectionist thinking patterns and develop cognitive diffusion from unhelpful thoughts.
2. **Finding Flow to Interrupt Anxiety:** Identifies and accesses flow states to reduce perfectionist overthinking and reconnect with present-moment engagement.
3. **"I Am" Identity Boards:** Builds authentic self-concept through visual exploration of personal values and qualities beyond performance measures.

Core takeaway: Shift from **perfect** to **progress + values**.

2 | The Thief of Comparison

The trap of measuring up

> "Don't compare your life to others. There's no comparison between the sun and the moon. They shine when it's their time."
>
> Anon.

Ben's story

In his early 20s, Ben's story mirrors the experience of many young graduates starting their professional careers in the social media-driven 2020s. Ben and I started working together around six months after he had graduated from a business degree from a well-regarded university in South Wales shortly after the COVID pandemic. Ben had been working part-time from his parental home in the southeast of England as a retail call centre operator, a job he had begun in the second year of his studies. It revealed his strong ability to build effective relationships and win round even the most disgruntled of customers.

His first foray into the world of graduate employment was recruitment-related, competitive and relentless. It did not take him long to realise that this first graduate job was not right for him. Knowing he had made the wrong choice was badly affecting his confidence and ability to move forward.

What struck me immediately during our initial conversation was the hesitation in his voice when discussing his career aspirations – not the uncertainty of someone exploring options, but the wariness of someone who had been burned before.

The experience was casting a long shadow over his ability to progress as he was worried about getting it wrong this time round too.

The more we worked together, the more Ben opened up. It became clear that the wrong graduate job was not his only unhelpful experience of the workplace, and his latest experience had a compounding effect on his confidence and self-worth. "I just don't want people to think I'm bad at my job," he said. "That's the big fear." We explored where this sense of fear came from, and slowly a pattern began to emerge. At school, he had occasionally been in lower sets and had often felt judged for not performing at the level of his peers. "It wasn't bullying," he told me. "It was just boys being boys. But there was always a comparison – always that sense of where you stood."

This sense of social comparison had followed him into university, where he had hoped things would be different. "It wasn't as snobby," he said, "but people still compared grades. You couldn't help but notice." When he got a 2:2, he felt deeply disappointed. "It's stuck with me, to be honest. I didn't feel good enough."

Ben's experience working in recruitment had compounded this feeling. He had a love of sports and, therefore, winning, and was good with people, so recruitment seemed like a logical step: fast-paced, people-focused, full of opportunity. But he lasted only a short while. "I hated it," he said bluntly. "It was all about numbers – targets, deals, comparisons. I was constantly looking over my shoulder. I'd only just started, and everyone else was already smashing it. I felt like a failure every day." With a father who represented the antithesis of competition, this constant competitive culture seemed alien to Ben.

Ben's discomfort was clear when he talked about the work and the environment. "It was the comparison," he realised. "The constant measuring. The sense that you're never enough." Through our conversation, Ben was able to connect this insight to his earlier experiences. At school, university and in his first job, the thread was always the same: performance equated to worth.

******

So, what is comparison?

The American Psychological Association defines comparison as *"the proposition that people evaluate their abilities and attitudes in relation to those of others in a process that plays a significant role in self-image and subjective wellbeing."*

From an OCEAN personality perspective, **Neuroticism** increases the frequency and negative emotional impact of social comparison, especially upward comparison. **Extraversion** is associated with a more positive, self-improving use of comparison, with extraverts preferring downward comparisons over upward ones compared to introverts. Both self-consciousness and low self-esteem make individuals more likely to engage in and be affected by comparison, as in Ben's case.

Competitiveness serves both as a cause and a consequence of frequent ability-based social comparison. Those with high achievement motivation (nAch) use social comparison frequently for self-evaluation and goal-setting. When the gap between current position and goals is moderate, this creates a motivational push to close it. When the gap feels too large, high achievers may disengage and give up.

Comparison becomes a thief when it shifts from healthy benchmarking to a constant internal monologue of inadequacy where individuals perceive they are behind others.

Why should we be worried about comparison?

Social comparison provides a way of comparing worth and progress when no definitive measures exist. We use it to reduce uncertainty, clarify where we stand and facilitate social connection by helping us fit in, understand norms and relate to others. From an evolutionary perspective, it helps us learn from others, survive and adapt within social groups.

As media, particularly social media, pervades our lives, we are increasingly surrounded by curated images of "perfect" lives, bodies and achievements. We mainly compare ourselves on abilities/skills, achievements/success, income/financial status, physical appearance, social status/popularity, personality traits and progress towards goals.

Psychology researcher Elaine Hatfield talks about *emotional contagion* – the automatic process where emotions spread between people through non-verbal cues. In social media contexts, the emotional tone of online content directly influences our mood and self-perception.

This content creates unrealistic standards and the impression that perfection is attainable and necessary. Individuals with depressive symptoms and poor self-esteem are more likely to engage in harmful social comparisons online, potentially worsening their mental health through passive consumption.

While social media comparison does not inherently cause neuroticism, it acts as a catalyst, exacerbating neurotic traits in susceptible individuals. The highlight-reel nature creates feedback loops that intensify emotional instability and fuel perfectionism. Social comparison also correlates with bullying, with upward comparisons fuelling envy and frustration.

Over-comparison can harm decision-making and lead to disconnection and isolation. As researchers Verduyn et al. have identified, social networking sites have amplified the frequency of social comparisons, often resulting in negative impacts on subjective wellbeing.

In the **workplace**, social comparison also plays a significant role, influencing motivation, teamwork, health and moral behaviour. It exists between employees, teams and firms. In a positive context, it can encourage individuals to pursue goals, work on themselves, foster team chemistry and follow the lead of others who change employers. However, it can also cause negative consequences such as jealousy and ego depletion, a form of loss of emotional self-control, which can lead to hiding knowledge, cyberloafing (a type of time theft relating to internet usage that is not related to one's job or academic responsibilities), poor work performance, absenteeism and even resignation. Negative social comparisons can also damage relationships, trust and job satisfaction. The success of the person comparing can have both positive and negative effects. Organisational contexts, such as limited resources, clear performance objectives and competitive incentive systems, can influence the emotional and behavioural effects of social comparison. Psychological resources also play a role, with employees who are more psychologically aware more likely to use comparison to improve themselves.

In **education**, as Ben's experiences reflect, students compare academic performance with classmates, which in turn shapes their academic self-concept and aspirations. Known as the "Big-Fish-Little-Pond Effect," a frame of reference model developed by Marsh and Parker in 1984, it indicates that being a top student in a lower-achieving school boosts academic self-concept more than being a lower-ranked student in a high-achieving school. This can influence self-belief, academic aspirations and performance, casting a shadow on career aspirations, ambitions and success later on. It is a direct contributor to performance anxiety.

When it comes to **age**, social comparison in young people is often driven by self-evaluation, self-improvement and the desire for social acceptance. As well as shaping beliefs, attitudes and self-identity, it can also increase vulnerability to negative emotions such as envy, inadequacy and anxiety, leading to mental health challenges. According to a 2023 report by the Cybersmile Foundation, 93% of 16–24-year-olds in the UK feel pressure to compare themselves with others online, with almost 60% doing so on a daily basis. Almost 90% felt unsatisfied with their life when comparing it to the lives of others on social media. Half of those surveyed experienced low self-esteem as a result and, perhaps most worrying of all, 14% had suicidal thoughts because of comparing themselves with others.

As the first generation growing up in a technologically advanced AI-driven world, **Generation Alpha** takes a unique approach. They are more varied and globally linked, comparing themselves to people from various backgrounds and cultures through influencers, peers and gamification on platforms which emphasise visual content. As a result of their global digital connectivity, they are more environmentally and socially conscious, emphasising activism, sustainability and social ideals. They are more likely to compare employers and career paths based on alignment with their values and the perceived social responsibility of organisations. Purpose-driven work and visible commitment to social causes will be major factors in their career decisions and satisfaction. This digital-native comparison has a mental health impact, including increased anxiety and reduced attention span which is likely to make project work, pace, variety, challenge and recognition appealing. In later life, the motivation to compare shifts towards self-protection, normalisation of age-related changes and maintaining self-esteem. Older adults tend to use comparison less for self-improvement and more for self-consistency and emotional regulation.

From a **gender** perspective, while everyone is prone to social comparison, women are generally more likely to compare, particularly when it comes to appearance and relationships. This comparison serves to make women more self-critical, negatively impacting our self-esteem and generating greater anxiety. In contrast, men typically compare less frequently, are likely to be less self-critical in their comparisons and are more likely to compare themselves to their own potential or future selves in a semi-hopeful or self-enhancing way. The impact of social comparison on men is often less negative, and others' outcomes have less effect on them.

Neurodivergent individuals often experience social comparison differently due to cognitive and social processing differences. They frequently perceive social cues differently, resulting in varying social comparison outcomes. While they show resilience to envy or upward comparisons, systemic stigma and masking behaviours can exacerbate mental health challenges. Long-term stress from discrimination can exacerbate negative social comparisons, resulting in mental health inequalities and leading to low self-esteem, while positive outcomes include in-group affirmation and redefining success.

Social comparison and socio-economic status (SES) are closely linked, influencing how people perceive their social standing, wellbeing and behaviour. Income inequality creates a culture of upward comparison, leading to status-based consumption and unhappiness, especially among lower earners. People use social signals like wealth, education and job status to determine their place in the social hierarchy, with SES affecting both comparison targets and social identity. Subjective SES and social comparison are better predictors of wellbeing than objective income. Upward comparisons can worsen self-perception and health, while downward comparisons provide temporary relief and self-enhancement. Strong SES-based identities foster community belonging but can also create social conflict and marginalisation.

From a **cultural perspective**, collectivist cultures (many Asian, Latin American and African countries) emphasise group harmony and modesty, fostering frequent comparison focused on self-improvement and group norm adherence. Individualistic, looser cultures (US, Canada, Western Europe) prioritise independence and uniqueness, with comparison motivated by self-enhancement rather than group harmony. In modesty-focused cultures like Scandinavia, individuals monitor themselves against others to avoid appearing arrogant, prioritising humility over self-promotion.

Comparison and sectors

Given technology and social media have heightened the dynamics of social comparison, it is prevalent across all industries, though its form, frequency and impact vary according to the culture, structures, performance structures and competitive dynamics within each sector. Social comparison explains more variance in financial satisfaction and anxiety than objective factors like income or education.

Motivations for comparison vary across different sectors based on culture:

- **High-competition sectors** such as **finance, sales, law, tech** and **consulting** experience more intense comparison, leading to motivation and stress.
- In **"tight," highly regulated sectors** like **healthcare, education, government** and **manufacturing**, comparison is a powerful force for conformity and rivalry.
- In **looser organisational cultures** like **engineering, research, nonprofits** and **project management organisations**, where collaboration is highly valued, comparison can be a source of inspiration and growth with a focus on collaboration, contribution to team goals and peer recognition. In corporate organisations, however, internal social comparison has a greater influence on strategic decisions and change than external comparison with other firms, especially in organisations with less-developed market institutions or more hierarchical, state-owned structures.

When it comes to **entrepreneurs**, comparison motivates them to set higher goals, benchmark progress, learn from role models and boost resilience, but it can also trigger stress, envy, reduced teamwork and emotional challenges in competitive environments.

Comparison across the career lifespan

As achievers move through the different career stages, their reasons for comparison alter:

Early careers: Graduate comparison is rife and can fuel difficulties with decision-making. Younger employees often compare themselves to older, more experienced colleagues who typically hold higher status and have more organisational tenure. This upward comparison can be motivating but may also be discouraging if the status gap feels insurmountable. If younger employees perceive that, regardless of effort, they cannot "catch up" to senior colleagues, their motivation and development striving may decrease.

Mid-careers: At this point, social comparison focuses on lateral peers, comparing job titles, lifestyle markers and children's achievements. While it can serve as a benchmark for competition or collaboration, it often creates career frustration, doubt and regret about perceived missed opportunities. Individuals may feel they have underperformed compared to peers, even when personally content. A strong vocational identity and clear career values can moderate these negative effects, providing protection against comparison-induced regret.

Late careers and retirement: Older professionals may compare themselves to rising younger colleagues, potentially reducing their motivation to mentor if they feel their expertise is becoming less valued. However, when older workers perceive similarity with younger colleagues, comparison becomes more existential, driving a desire to leave a legacy and enhancing motivation to share knowledge.

The neuroscience of comparison

The "common currency hypothesis" explains how our brain processes comparison information by placing different types of rewards and losses – social (praise, superiority) and non-social (money) – on the same mental measuring scale, allowing direct comparison of different experiences.

When clients engage in comparison, four key brain systems activate in distinct patterns depending on whether they're comparing upwards (to those "better off") or downwards (to those "worse off"): pain circuits (registering social threat), reward circuits (seeking status and dopamine from superiority), executive function systems (attempting rational control), and social cognition networks (hyperactively scanning others' success). Upward comparisons activate the same pain circuits as physical injury and impair executive function. Recovery requires limbic regulation first, then cognitive restructuring. This explains why telling clients to "just stop comparing" fails as their rational brain cannot override four simultaneous neurological systems designed for survival and reward-seeking.

Brain chemistry

The brain chemistry behind comparison involves key neurotransmitters working together, making comparison behaviours neurochemically addictive over time. Dopamine drives reward feelings during downward comparisons, serotonin influences how we process social fairness, and oxytocin can reduce competitive focus by promoting connection and empathy.

To counteract clients' neurological responses, practitioners need to:

- help calm the emotional brain first,
- enhance psychological safety to overcome the real pain of criticism,
- support full executive functioning recovery before resuming coaching conversations, and
- work overtime to break the addictive achievement reward system.

The activities that follow help overcome these impacts on the brain system, and align well with the main comparison theories covered in this chapter.

Comparison theory in action

Ben's story shows how social comparison can quietly corrode self-belief. By looking at his own words, we can see how the main theories intersect to explain the emotional, cognitive and behavioural impact of comparison on his early career.

"There was always a comparison - always that sense of where you stood"

From school onwards, Ben described a constant backdrop of comparison:

- **Festinger's Social Comparison Theory** explains how individuals evaluate themselves by comparing to others when objective standards are lacking. Ben gauged his self-worth through peers' performance in class sets, degree classifications and early job results.
- **Stouffer's Relative Deprivation Theory** shows how feeling "just behind" slightly better-off peers fosters resentment or discouragement. Though he had a good degree and skills, Ben still felt disadvantaged, internalising comparison as inadequacy.

Together, these theories reveal how early patterns of comparison became embedded, shaping how Ben measured his worth throughout his education and career.

"I didn't feel good enough"

Ben's 2:2 result became a defining moment: despite graduating, he experienced it as proof of failure.

- **Tesser's Self-Evaluation Maintenance Theory** suggests that close peers' success in identity-relevant domains (grades, job performance) threatened Ben's self-esteem.
- **Kahneman and Tversky's Prospect Theory** explains how losses are felt more strongly than equivalent gains. Missing a 2:1 carried disproportionate emotional weight, overshadowing the achievement of graduating.
- **Stouffer's Relative Deprivation Theory** adds that the sense of being slightly worse off than peers magnified his disappointment.

These theories show why Ben's conclusion, *"I'm not good enough,"* carried such enduring power.

"I just don't want people to think I'm bad at my job"

Ben's fear of judgement reflects the corrosive link between comparison and identity.

- **Clance and Imes's imposter syndrome (Perceived Fraudulence Theory)** highlights how individuals attribute success externally and live in fear of exposure. Despite his strong interpersonal skills and positive feedback, Ben doubted his ability to sustain success.
- **Self-Discrepancy Theory** (see Chapter 1) provides a useful lens: Ben's ought-self demanded that others perceive him as competent, creating anxiety whenever he fell short of this internalised obligation.

Here, comparison produced not just disappointment but a persistent fear of being seen as inadequate, reinforcing avoidance and hesitation in his career choices.

**"It was the comparison. The constant measuring.
The sense that you're never enough"**

This final statement captures the Thief of Comparison most starkly.

- In recruitment, the constant ranking by numbers, targets and deals amplified his insecurities.
- Organisational research shows that competitive incentive systems heighten upward comparison, fuelling stress, disengagement and self-doubt.
- Ben's reflection illustrates how comparison can tip from healthy benchmarking into toxic erosion of confidence, particularly in high-pressure, target-driven environments.

What Ben's story shows us

Ben's phrases reveal how comparison shapes identity and wellbeing across settings. *"There was always a comparison"* shows how early habits of measuring up became ingrained. *"I didn't feel good enough"* highlights the lasting impact of academic benchmarks, intensified by loss aversion. *"I just don't want people to think I'm bad at my job"* exposes how fear of judgement and imposter feelings corrode confidence. Finally, *"It was the comparison... the sense that you're never enough"* names the thief directly, showing how competitive contexts magnify vulnerability. Together, these words demonstrate three key insights:

- **Comparison entrenches identity wounds early**, shaping career confidence for years.
- **Upward comparison intensifies loss aversion**, making setbacks loom larger than achievements.
- **Competitive contexts amplify imposter fears**, leaving achievers vulnerable to chronic self-doubt and disengagement.

Ben's case illustrates that comparison does more than measure performance: it threatens self-worth and obscures authentic motivation.

In the next section, we will explore how coaching helped Ben reframe comparison, strengthen self-acceptance and make career choices guided by authenticity rather than fear.

Decoding and resolving Ben's comparison tendencies

The pivotal moment in our work came when I asked Ben, "When it's a competitive, comparative environment, what's going to happen to your brain when you're there?"

"It's just going to go back to all those bad thoughts," Ben realised. "It will prove you're right to be worried."

The question helped Ben to connect his current thinking with his experiences and emotions.

"I hadn't really thought about comparing those two things," he said, reflecting on the similarities between his school experience and recruitment role. "But thinking about it now, recruitment was very comparative all the time... And I hated that."

We talked about what environments did matter to him. When he talked about college, he lit up: "It was different. Less competitive. More about getting on with your own thing." That was a clue. He thrived in collaborative, supportive environments – not combative ones.

To help him trust himself and make an authentic choice that would work for him, regardless of others, we reviewed his skills and mapped them to the kinds of roles that excited him. Ben was particularly interested in PR.

He began to see a pattern of strengths – and where he was most energised. "I love writing. I love sport. I like working with people. I'm good at that."

He liked the idea of being part of a team, using his writing skills and working in an area he cared about. "It's fast-paced," he said, "but it's more collaborative. You're working on projects together."

We reviewed the work we had done earlier on values to ensure that the direction Ben was keen to progress in aligned authentically.

By the end of our session, Ben looked lighter. "I think I've found it," he said. "It just makes sense now." Through conversation, he had been able to reframe his earlier experiences not as failures but as signposts. Recruitment had not been a failure. It had shown him what kind of environment he needed to avoid. It was, in his words, "a blessing in disguise."

Ben's story illustrates how social comparison and imposter syndrome quietly corrode self-belief, particularly for high achievers. Though Ben loved to succeed, comparison had robbed him of achievement joy and clouded decision-making by prioritising others' opinions over what truly energised him. His brain had been trained to associate professional environments with judgement, creating unconscious fear responses affecting career choices.

Through coaching, Ben reduced the gap between actual and ought-self by realigning career choices with his interests and strengths. He reframed perceived failures as directional insight (recruitment wasn't wrong, just misaligned), reconnected with authentic motivation ("I think I've found it... it just makes sense now"), and shifted from fear-driven comparison to values-driven career alignment. He is now pursuing sports PR, having secured work experience with a London agency.

*****

Using the ABCDE model to help Ben move forward

Activating event

Ben's struggled in his first graduate job in recruitment. In a highly competitive environment, surrounded by fast-performing peers, he experienced old, familiar feelings of not measuring up, which echoed his earlier experiences at school and university.

Cognitive biases, dissonance and **distortion at play** were underpinned by his upward comparison bias where he focused on those outperforming him. This led him to overlook his strengths and progress and concentrate on perceived shortcomings.

Somatic markers were evident in key moments of our discussion. The various breaks in eye contact, colour shifts in his face, a quieter voice and a drop of the head and shoulders in his responses revealed anxiety and shame over previous failures.

Beliefs

These were clear in his statements such as: *"Performance equals worth,"* *"Others will think I'm bad at my job if I don't succeed quickly,"* *"If I fail again, it proves I'm not good enough,"* and *"Success is about keeping up or staying ahead."* It was clear that it was Ben's clearly held beliefs, shaped by a lifetime of comparison, which had led him to experience reduced self-esteem and self-belief.

Consequences

These beliefs and comparisons had significant consequences for Ben. Emotionally, he displayed low confidence, fear of failure and a well-masked underlying anxiety connected with feeling like he was an imposter. Behaviourally, he was hesitant in his decision-making and had opted to leave the role because of its competitive nature. Cognitively, he had found it difficult to trust his own career instincts. Ben's constant self-monitoring and comparison made it hard for him to move forward with clarity or confidence.

Dispute

Through coaching, I encouraged Ben to explore whether the competitive recruitment culture had been right for him. Using the metaphor of a rose needing the right soil to grow, he recognised that recruitment was simply the wrong environment. This created space between his past experience and hope for better fit, boosting his confidence.

I helped him identify the *"work soil"* he would flourish in and asked whether comparison was helping or holding him back. This separated his ability from his unhappiness in an unsuitable environment. Having identified his strengths in writing and phone-based relationships, we explored PR in detail so he could connect context, skills and impact. He began distinguishing external expectations from internal motivation, recognising that distress stemmed from misalignment, not failure. This reframing allowed a more compassionate and authentic self-view to emerge.

Effect

Once Ben recognised that his distress stemmed from misalignment rather than failure, he adopted a new belief centred on authentic alignment over external validation. Rather than chasing others' definitions of success, he began trusting that fulfilment comes from working in spaces aligned with his strengths (writing, communication, teamwork), sports interests and values – collaborative, meaningful and less comparison-driven.

The PR role he targeted offers purpose and connection relating to who he is and wants to be, rather than performance metrics alone. To test his thinking, I encouraged him to start a sports newsletter on Substack, enabling him to experience sports writing and build a portfolio for future employers.

As a result of our coaching sessions over time, Ben was able to gain clarity about what really mattered to him, through becoming crystal clear about his values. Using those as a lens on career choice helped him to know he was making the right choice for him and not snatching at an alternative.

He is now actively seeking roles in PR, where his talents, interests and values align – a shift from fear-based avoidance to values-based, future-facing action.

Activities to create changes in comparison thinking and behaviour

Ben's story is about his journey towards self-acceptance and feeling comfortable in his own skin. In a culture where comparison has become second nature, self-acceptance is a powerful tool to mitigate comparison's impact. Instead of chasing the endless goal of being better than everyone else, self-acceptance offers a more self-compassionate path.

While self-esteem fluctuates with successes and failures, particularly when compared to others, self-acceptance enables us to recognise and value our inherent worth. This provides a stable foundation to acknowledge all of our unique story, whether strengths, limitations, achievements or mistakes, as key parts of the human experience.

Research shows those with higher self-acceptance experience less distress from upward social comparisons, feeling inspired rather than diminished by others' achievements. This stability reflects what psychologist Carol Ryff described as a core pillar of psychological wellbeing – a realistic, accepting attitude towards oneself (for more on this see Chapter 7).

As Carl Rogers observed, "The curious paradox is that when I accept myself just as I am, then I can change." Self-acceptance redirects attention from external comparison to internal exploration, creating space for clients to discover who they truly are. As comparison becomes less triggering, so resilience can grow and support clients to write their own unique story.

Deci and Ryan's Self-Determination Theory shows self-acceptance loosens comparison's grip by supporting three core psychological needs:

- autonomy (feeling self-directed),
- competence (feeling effective), and
- relatedness (feeling connected).

The three activities which follow develop these needs, reducing comparison's impact.

ACTIVITY 1: CREATING A LIFE VALUES COMPASS

In a world of noise, it is easy to get distracted from what really matters to us. This two-part exercise helps clients to identify the values which intrinsically motivate them in every area of their lives and evaluate how well their values are expressed over time.

To start with, ask your client to review the eight segments of the Life Values Compass below. (Some clients may want to create their own version with more or fewer segments.)

Then ask them to identify the values that matter most to them in each segment.

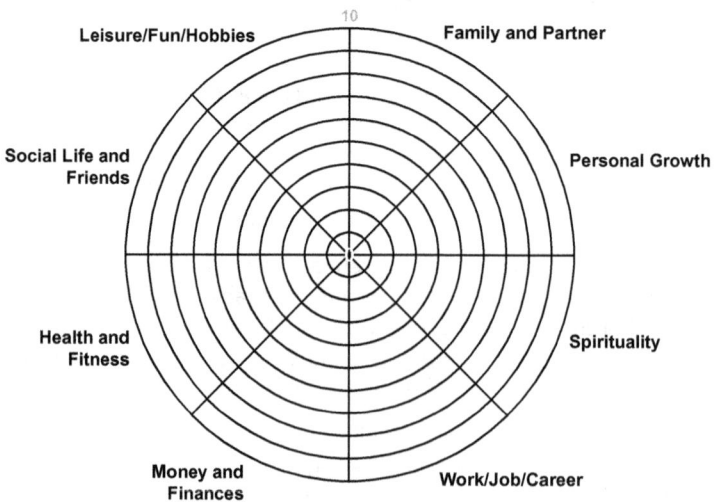

This activity is available for download from Trotman's website, so clients can write the top three values in each segment. To access, use the QR code or visit the web address at the start of this book.

As a work-related example, values might include autonomy, contribution/making a difference, creativity, challenge, teamwork or recognition. As a family-related example, typical values might include loyalty, love, communication, support or togetherness.

You may need to prompt their thinking using questions such as:

* *"What would make this area feel rich or meaningful?"*
* *"What principles guide how you want to be in this area of your life?"*
* *"What frustrates you here – and what does that tell you about what you value?"*

Once your client has identified their top values in each segment, ask them to rate how well they are currently living those values on a 0–10 scale. Asking a client to shade in their current score in each segment will highlight where there are areas which they would benefit from further reflection and coaching.

Once completed, this activity provides the backdrop for you to work with your client to identify and resolve:

* Segments where values are being neglected or suppressed.
* Value conflicts between segments (e.g. work v. health).
* Hidden sources of discontent that are not about performance, but misalignment.

It is helpful for the client if they revisit this document every quarter so they can review their values and progress made.

ACTIVITY 2: DEVELOPING A CLIENT'S "SIGNATURE BLEND"

Just as different brands of coffee have their own unique signature blend, so do we all. This competence recognition activity helps clients shift their focus from comparing themselves to others towards recognising and owning their own unique capabilities, strengths and talents.

From a psychological perspective, the American Psychological Association defines competence as: *"the ability to exert control over one's life, to cope with specific problems effectively, and to make changes to one's behavior and one's environment, as opposed to the mere ability to adjust or adapt to circumstances as they are."* From a career perspective, the ESCO (European Skills, Competences, Qualifications and Occupations), the European multilingual classification of Skills, Competences and Occupations defines competence as *"the proven ability to use knowledge, skills and personal, social and/or methodological abilities, in work or study situations and in professional and personal development."*

I use a simple model I created called ASKE with my clients to help my clients understand what they have to offer and build their unique profile confidently. ASKE stands for Attributes (attitude/aptitude), Skills, Knowledge and Experience and matches the four areas employers seek when recruiting. The image below shows the model in action.

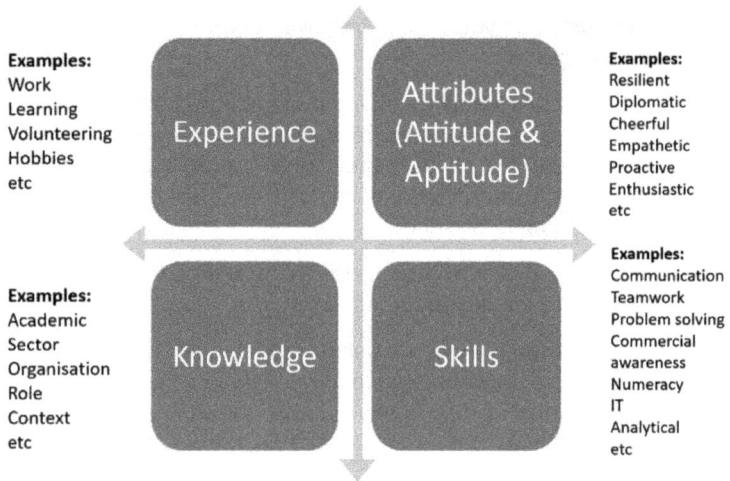

Examples:
Work
Learning
Volunteering
Hobbies
etc

Experience

Attributes (Attitude & Aptitude)

Examples:
Resilient
Diplomatic
Cheerful
Empathetic
Proactive
Enthusiastic
etc

Examples:
Communication
Teamwork
Problem solving
Commercial
awareness
Numeracy
IT
Analytical
etc

Examples:
Academic
Sector
Organisation
Role
Context
etc

Knowledge

Skills

To begin, ask the client to focus on one box at a time and identify all the different elements of competence in that area. Then ask them to find examples of these qualities/competencies in action and identify their best example of each. The next step is to ask them to score the individual competence/quality out of five, where five is high, both in terms of ability and enjoyment. Each of these steps provides an opportunity for you to help the client to evaluate, contextualise and recognise their qualities and abilities.

One question to ask as part of this is: *"What do you do so easily that you can't understand why others can't do it?"* This will enable you both to identify and discuss their natural talents, which will help reinforce intrinsic understanding and motivations. You could also ask questions such as *"Which of these competencies do you tend to undervalue because they come naturally to you?"* and *"Where do you find yourself comparing your abilities to others rather than appreciating your unique combination?"*

When clients clearly see what they offer, on their terms, they are less likely to seek self-worth through comparison. Instead, they can recognise the quiet brilliance in what comes naturally to them and whatever else is in their competence store cupboard or inventory.

If your client has already completed the Life Values Compass activity, you can use it to help them explore how their highest-scoring ASKE strengths align with their core values. This step helps them see the connection between who they are, what they are good at and what really matters to them. When there is clarity about who we are, the need for comparison to make us feel better abates. Completing the first two exercises will help clients to recognise and develop their "signature blend."

ACTIVITY 3: COMPARING APPROPRIATELY

To enable clients to benefit from healthy social media engagement, we need to help them develop the ability to distinguish between dopamine-driven and values-driven interactions. Dopamine-driven engagement creates a predictable pattern of physical sensations including compulsive reaching for devices, restless scrolling despite feeling unsatisfied, tension or anxiety when disconnected and shallow breathing during extended sessions. Social media platforms leverage the same neural circuitry used by slot machines and drugs, creating dopamine deficits where users need increasingly intense digital experiences to achieve satisfaction, leading to a cycle of escalating use with diminishing returns.

In contrast, values-driven engagement produces expansive bodily sensations such as a more intentional approach to device use, a sense of calm expansion when viewing meaningful content, natural breathing patterns and feeling energised rather than drained after use. This increases intrinsic versus extrinsic motivation, where values-driven engagement supports autonomy, competence and relatedness, while dopamine-driven engagement undermines these fundamental psychological needs through external validation seeking.

Helping clients develop their sense of **embodied awareness** enables them to make wise choices so that social media works for them rather not against them. Embodied awareness is the capacity to notice, interpret and respond to one's internal experience, whether thoughts, emotions or sensations, as they arise in the body. It involves being fully present, not only mentally but physically and emotionally, using the body as a source of insight, grounding and self-regulation. This process draws on interoception – the ability to perceive internal bodily signals such as heartbeat, breathing and gut sensations, which provides crucial information for decision-making and emotional regulation. Unlike abstract reflection, embodied awareness anchors awareness in a client's felt experience of the present moment. It helps them connect with their intuition, regulate their nervous system and make more aligned decisions. This is particularly valuable when navigating stress, uncertainty or disconnection.

Antonio Damasio's groundbreaking somatic marker hypothesis provides a well-established scientific foundation for understanding how our bodies guide decision-making processes, including social media choices. Somatic markers are feelings in the body associated with emotions that strongly influence decision-making. These bodily responses become associated with particular situations and guide behaviour through both conscious and unconscious processes. When encountering social media content, our bodies generate immediate somatic responses – subtle changes in heart rate, breathing, muscle tension or gut feelings – that signal whether the content aligns with our values and wellbeing. These "marker" signals influence response processes at multiple levels, some occurring consciously and others unconsciously, arising from bioregulatory processes that express themselves through emotions and feelings. By developing awareness of these somatic markers, clients can use their body's wisdom as a real-time feedback system, allowing contractive sensations such as tension, shallow breathing and agitation to signal dopamine-driven engagement while expansive sensations including openness, calm energy and inspiration indicate values-driven interaction. This embodied approach transforms social media from a passive consumption experience into an active, body-informed curation practice that supports authentic self-expression and genuine connection.

This holistic activity helps clients avoid the comparison trap by developing embodied awareness to distinguish between dopamine-driven and values-driven social media engagement. Using their body's wisdom as a real-time feedback system, clients can learn to curate their social media experience consciously, ensuring it supports rather than undermines their wellbeing and authentic self-expression.

Step 1: Body awareness mapping

To help your client tune into their emotional awareness, ask your client to draw two outlines of a body or provide them with one. Then ask them to think about a time when they felt really happy. Then ask them to describe what they feel and where the centre of that feeling is on their body, what they are thinking and what is happening with their physiology including breathing, heart rate and muscular tension. Encourage them to capture what they experienced on the body chart.

Now repeat the activity, this time asking them to think of a time when they felt somewhat unhappy and again notice their thinking, feeling and physiological responses. Make sure they do not pick a significant negative emotional event, just something big enough that they can notice their reaction to it. Encourage your client to capture their responses on the second body outline once they have identified them.

Then work with your client to help them notice the contrast in their thinking, embodied feelings and physiological responses by comparing the two states. This will bring to their awareness what has likely been unconscious reactions. Being aware of these responses will help them break any cycle of doom-scrolling and tipping into comparison mode.

Step 2. Social media emotional response audit

Next, ask your client to spend 15 minutes or so looking at their favourite social media account, noticing their positive and more stressed embodied awareness reactions to posts as they scroll through. Once they have done this, they will be able to identify positive and negative triggers. This can be done together or by the client alone.

Step 3. Values and signature blend check

The final step is to work together to help the client identify how positive responses relate to their Life Values Compass and Signature Blend. Doing so helps to create a strategy for knowing who and what to follow that supports their wellbeing and growth and who and what to delete to reduce opportunities for negative comparison. This can be developed into a personal social media strategy which brings both growth and opportunity.

Summary

As you will have discovered, the Thief of Comparison is a danger to our wellbeing, authenticity and ability to progress. By helping clients understand and recognise comparison in action through becoming aware and intrinsically motivated, we can help them navigate an increasingly noisy world effectively and mitigate the impact of that noise. The primary underlying fears and behaviours which social comparison triggers can leave us and our clients feeling less worthy and worthwhile. When at full tilt, social comparison inevitably provokes feelings of inadequacy, causing us to turn to others for reassurance. The Thief of Approval-Seeking provides the theme for the next chapter.

2. The Thief of Comparison
At a glance

Definition: "The proposition that people evaluate their abilities and attitudes in relation to those of others in a process that plays a significant role in self-image and subjective wellbeing." (APA)

Key theories and models:

1. **Social Comparison Theory (Festinger, 1954):** People evaluate themselves by comparing themselves to others when objective standards are lacking, driving self-assessment and motivation.
2. **Self-Evaluation Maintenance Theory (Tesser, 1988):** Others' success boosts self-esteem in irrelevant domains but threatens it in valued ones, with closeness and relevance shaping impact.

Impact and context:

93% of 16–24-year-olds feel pressure to compare online; 60% do so daily.

90% feel unsatisfied when comparing lives on social media; 14% have suicidal thoughts.

Women compare more on appearance/relationships; men compare less frequently.

Comparison is high in finance, law, tech, sales; moderate in collaborative sectors.

- **Early career:** Decision-making difficulties.
- **Mid-career:** Lifestyle markers.
- **Late career:** Younger colleague comparison.

Warning signs:

- **Constant measuring:** Always checking where you stand relative to others.
- **Social media scrolling:** Compulsive checking of others' highlights reels.
- **Achievement anxiety:** Fear that others are progressing faster.
- **Imposter feelings:** "I don't belong here" despite evidence of competence.
- **Career FOMO:** Worry about missing opportunities others have.
- **Qualification inflation:** Feeling the need to over-credential compared to peers.
- **Success minimisation:** Downplaying achievements when others seem ahead.

The trap of measuring up

3. **Perceived Fraudulence Theory/Imposter Phenomenon (Clance and Imes, 1978):** Persistent self-doubt despite success, linking imposter feelings to perfectionism and fear of exposure in competitive environments.
4. **Prospect Theory (Kahneman and Tversky, 1979):** People judge outcomes relative to reference points, with losses weighing more than gains, magnifying comparative setbacks.
5. **Relative Deprivation Theory (Stouffer, 1949):** Feelings of disadvantage arise from comparisons with slightly better-off peers, where subjective inequality fuels dissatisfaction.

Neuroscience:

Comparison activates four key brain systems differently based on upward versus downward comparison:

- **Pain circuits:** Upward comparisons activate the same pathways as physical injury.
- **Reward circuits:** Downward comparisons trigger dopamine release.
- **Executive function:** Impaired during upward comparison stress.
- **Social cognition:** Hyperactive scanning of others' success.

Neurochemically addictive patterns develop where downward comparison provides temporary relief, reinforcing the need to compare.

Key coaching activities:

1. **Life Values Compass:** Map authentic values across life domains to redirect focus from external comparison to internal alignment.
2. **Signature Blend:** Identify and develop a unique combination of abilities and strengths to build confidence through distinctive contribution.
3. **Embodied Awareness:** Use body wisdom to distinguish between dopamine-driven and values-driven online engagement patterns.

Core takeaway: Shift from **measuring up** to **showing up authentically**.

3 | The Thief of Approval-Seeking

Acting to please others

> "It takes courage to grow up and become who you really are."
> EE Cummings, American poet, painter, author and playwright.

Amir's story

Amir was quite stuck when he came for some coaching at the instigation of his mother, Priya, who had got in touch. During the discovery call with both Priya and Amir, it was clear that Amir needed help to move forward. A bright, thoughtful graduate with a 2:2 in engineering from a prestigious Russell Group university, he found himself spending his days working in a coffee shop, drifting between shifts and uncertainty. On paper, he had plenty going for him: strong interpersonal skills, a solid degree and a significant number of high-quality relevant work placements. Yet despite these, he was clearly wrestling with something far more complex, which we explored later during our sessions.

Raised in a high-achieving family where academic success and professional status were deeply valued, Amir had followed a path that on the surface seemed right, but the deeper he got into it, the less it did not feel like his own. His mother, Priya, held a senior role in a prestigious investment firm, and his father was equally established in his field. They had made sacrifices, worked hard and built a life of opportunity for their two sons. Naturally, they hoped Amir and his younger brother would follow a similarly successful trajectory.

From a young age, the message was clear: engineering was a good, respectable and appropriate path. So, Amir followed the path. He completed placements in engineering, satellite technology and clean energy. His CV reflected a young man preparing to launch a promising career.

But that was not how he felt. It was more that there was an internal tug of war going on between who he believed he was expected to be and what actually spoke to him. As a way of finding solace, on days when he was not working, Amir took to the kitchen, where he spent time inventing dishes for his family to enjoy as they discussed events from everyone's day.

By the time he graduated, engineering left Amir feeling drained. He suspected he might be dyslexic, although it had gone undiagnosed throughout his studies. Even more significant was the lack of connection to the subject itself. "I love to achieve," he confided. "But during my degree, I just couldn't find the drive. Though some of it was hard, I wasn't failing because I couldn't do it, I was failing because I didn't want to." The only modules he genuinely enjoyed were in product design and new product development. "Those were my best marks," he said. "I actually got firsts in some of them."

His final degree grade, a lower division second class honours, felt like a failure, not just academically, but culturally. In his family, and extended community, grades mattered. Success stories were shared proudly around the table while struggles were endured quietly. For Amir, who had always aimed to make his parents proud, the weight of their unspoken disappointment was hard to carry.

What he hadn't fully voiced at first but gradually acknowledged as I explored his feelings with him was the deeper fear sitting underneath it all – the fear of being a disappointment. Amir wasn't just afraid of failure. He was afraid of falling short in their eyes. Beneath the surface was something more painful, the idea that if he didn't live up to the expectations set for him, he might lose their pride, their trust – and even, in some fragile way, their love. I asked him if he had any other fears. He replied in a quiet, worried voice, "Because I know that engineering isn't right for me, I am worried that I will never find what is and may never actually achieve my potential."

"They keep asking about my job applications," he said. "And I can see the concern and worry in their eyes when I don't have good news. I feel like I'm failing them again…"

Amir did not rebel or push back. Instead, like many who become conforming people-pleasers, he simply stalled. It became clear that for Amir, as with so many young adults whose identities and independence are still forming, letting them down felt simply too costly and too risky. So, he had taken refuge in something familiar and unthreatening – quiet avoidance, working barista shifts locally.

By the time he started coaching, Amir was headed for a professional life that looked respectable on paper, but which made him feel like he was locked in a golden cage, secure, looking polished and admired, but lacking in soul.

It was clear that he knew what was expected of him. But for the first time, he was beginning to wonder how he could find a way to something that would light him up and would love rather than endure.

*****

So, what is approval-seeking?

Unlike previous thieves, while there is no single universally approved definition of approval-seeking, there are widely accepted descriptions in clinical and coaching contexts. Broadly, therefore, approval-seeking is the habitual tendency to seek validation, acceptance or recognition from others, often at the expense of one's own needs, values or authenticity, in order to gain reassurance, avoid disapproval or maintain social harmony. Individuals seeking approval often face challenges such as disapproval, rejection and criticism, and struggle to trust their own judgement. They need validation before acting and doubt their worth without external praise. This behaviour is similar to comparison, where individuals seek external reassurance to restore self-worth. As we saw in the previous chapter, frequent social comparison leads to uncertainty about one's value, requiring validation from others to confirm worth.

From a personality perspective, using OCEAN as a lens, **Neuroticism** shows the strongest correlation with approval-seeking, as individuals high in this trait experience more anxiety, self-doubt and fear of negative evaluation. **Agreeableness** can contribute to approval-seeking through people-pleasing behaviours, though many agreeable people maintain healthy boundaries. **Conscientiousness** may involve seeking approval for work quality and achievement, particularly when combined with perfectionist tendencies. **Extraversion**'s relationship with approval-seeking is complex: while extraverts enjoy social validation, their social confidence often reduces dependency on approval. Finally, **Openness** shows the weakest correlation, as these individuals typically value authenticity and novel ideas over conventional approval.

Why should we be worried about approval-seeking?

A fundamental human drive, approval-seeking promotes social connection and belonging, achievement and adaptability. However, when it becomes a condition for self-worth, it undermines individual authenticity, mental health, autonomy, relationships and personal growth. Excessive approval-seeking increases anxiety, stress and lowers self-esteem, hindering authentic relationships and self-expression. It also makes it difficult to set boundaries and contributes to perfectionism and burnout. The transformation from healthy social motivation to a destructive thief occurs when our sense of worth is dependent on others' acceptance, stealing our capacity for authentic self-expression and autonomous decision-making.

In the **workplace**, approval-seeking can negatively impact wellbeing, decision-making, innovation and creativity, leadership and team dynamics. It increases burnout, overperformance and slows career progression. Withholding honest opinions can lead to groupthink and difficulty in making challenging decisions. Overworking and perfectionism can result in career stagnation. As we saw with Amir, excessive external validation reduces autonomy and intrinsic motivation, while constant self-monitoring can increase anxiety and reduce authenticity.

Approval-seeking in **education** affects students' motivation, academic behaviour, emotional wellbeing and achievement. It can lead to academic self-handicapping, procrastination and avoiding challenging tasks. As researchers have shown over time, there is a positive relationship between peer approval-seeking and academic self-handicapping behaviours. Emotional wellbeing can be affected by positive self-appraisals, while strong approval-seeking motives can hinder the development of self-regulatory skills. Balancing external validation with internal self-worth is crucial for educational success and wellbeing.

From an **age perspective**, approval-seeking is highest in childhood and adolescence, as self-concept formation is ongoing and there is particular sensitivity to social feedback. As individuals grow, they develop emotional regulation and identity. Approval-seeking may persist into early adulthood but declines as life experience and confidence increase. Middle-aged adults focus on internal values and self-acceptance, prioritising authenticity and emotional honesty over external validation. However, individuals who experienced conditional love, emotional neglect or inconsistent validation may continue this behaviour into adulthood.

When it comes to **gender**, differences in approval-seeking vary. Girls and women seek it more in social or relationship settings due to their connection-based values. Boys and men also seek approval for success, recognition or status. Women may feel extra pressure in male-dominated environments, especially in the workplace. It is worth remembering that approval-seeking motivations are influenced more by personal, cultural and contextual factors than by gender alone.

Neurodivergent individuals often exhibit intense approval-seeking behaviours due to social experiences, psychological patterns and neurological differences. This can lead to misunderstandings, criticism and exclusion, requiring external validation. Rejection Sensitive Dysphoria (RSD) in ADHD patients is known to cause emotional responses to perceived rejection, leading to people-pleasing behaviours and emotional exhaustion. This can lower self-esteem, creating cycles where approval-seeking becomes a survival strategy.

When it comes to **socio-economic status** (SES), approval-seeking behaviours are more prevalent among individuals from lower socio-economic backgrounds, especially in academic, workplace and social settings. This is due to lower self-esteem, reduced perceived control and increased sensitivity to social comparison. In environments with economic inequality or competitive hierarchies, approval-seeking may serve as a compensatory strategy. Higher SES individuals show more autonomy but may still seek approval in high-status environments. Cultural norms and early experiences influence these behaviours.

From a **cultural perspective**, approval-seeking varies across cultures and ethnic groups, with collectivist cultures reinforcing it more, while individualist cultures value independence and personal achievement. Minority individuals often seek approval to avoid discrimination, especially immigrants and bicultural individuals. Social media has amplified approval-seeking, making validation more visible and measurable. Both cultural norms and modern technologies influence how approval-seeking appears in different social and organisational settings.

Approval-seeking and sectors

A common behaviour in all industries, the intensity, expression and impact of approval-seeking varies depending on the sector. While moderate approval-seeking can foster collaboration and motivation, excessive reliance on external validation can erode autonomy, authenticity and psychological safety. Motivations for approval-seeking vary by sector context:

- **High-status, hierarchical sectors** like **finance, law, consulting** and **large corporations** often foster stronger approval-seeking tendencies to gain promotions, bonuses or prestige, leading to overwork, risk aversion and groupthink.
- **Customer-facing sectors** like **sales, hospitality, healthcare** and **teaching** also encourage approval-seeking through client feedback, ratings and relationship management, leading to people-pleasing behaviours, emotional exhaustion and blurred boundaries.
- **Creative and media sectors** often pursue public recognition, social media metrics or critical acclaim, but this can tie self-worth too closely to external opinions.
- **STEM and technical fields** such as **engineering**, **IT** and **research** tend to focus more on outcomes than praise, and approval-seeking is more contained in competitive academic environments or performance review cycles.
- **Nonprofit and mission-driven organisations** may encourage value-based alignment over personal advancement, but when unchecked, it can lead to overidentification, burnout or self-sacrifice to maintain belonging and purpose.

Approval-seeking becomes problematic when external validation replaces internal motivation as the primary measure of worth. When embedded in leadership cultures, it can shape decision-making, reduce innovation and hinder growth.

Approval-seeking in **entrepreneurship** can hinder risk-taking and innovation, as entrepreneurs may avoid bold ideas, delay decisions and conform to others' expectations. A fear of criticism can lead to safer ventures, while reassurance-seeking can undermine agility and resilience. Innovation thrives on experimentation, authenticity and a fail-forward approach, which approval-seeking can suppress. Successful entrepreneurs rely on internal confidence and purpose, allowing them to take calculated risks and pursue novel ideas.

Approval-seeking across the career lifespan

As professionals progress through different career stages, the function and intensity of approval-seeking shifts, shaped by identity development, workplace experience and evolving confidence.

Early careers: At this crucial stage of personal identity and career development, young professionals and achievers rely heavily on validation from managers, mentors and peers to build confidence and feel secure. Often highly attuned to how they are perceived, they adjust their behaviours to appear competent or high-potential. Career choices may reflect parental or societal expectations, with social comparison and the desire for approval driving early milestones.

Mid-careers: Here, approval-seeking becomes more selective and strategic as confidence and competence increase. Professionals balance external validation with internal success measures, particularly in competitive/hierarchical settings, and impression management is more targeted during transitions or promotions. In leadership roles, approval-seeking shifts from managers to teams, leading to consensus-seeking behaviours or people-pleasing to maintain harmony. At this stage, the fear of reputational damage, being "found out," or career stagnation can subtly sustain external validation needs, particularly for those in performance-driven cultures.

Late careers and retirement: By this point, approval-seeking tends to decline as individuals prioritise authenticity and meaningful work over external recognition. Impression management wanes as older professionals express their true views and focus on mentoring, legacy-building and respecting their experience and wisdom. The desire to contribute meaningfully often replaces the earlier drive to impress.

The neuroscience of approval-seeking

According to neuroscience research, social rewards, such as praise, acceptance and a sense of belonging, activate the same brain reward circuits as primary survival needs, including food and safety. This neurological overlap explains why approval-seeking behaviours can feel essential for survival, even when they compromise authenticity or wellbeing.

When clients engage in approval-seeking behaviour, the brain's established systems activate in a coordinated pattern, creating a powerful neurological drive. Understanding these patterns explains why simply telling someone to "stop seeking approval" is ineffective – the rational mind cannot override these deeply embedded survival and reward systems without targeted intervention.

During approval-seeking episodes, the reward system treats social validation as a primary survival need, flooding the brain with dopamine and creating reinforcing pursuit patterns. Simultaneously, the threat detection system interprets potential disapproval as genuine danger, activating the same neural pathways as physical pain. The social cognition network becomes hyperactive, constantly scanning and predicting others' responses, while the executive control system becomes compromised, impairing authentic decision-making and boundary-setting.

This coordinated activation creates a neurological perfect storm: clients simultaneously crave approval (reward system), fear disapproval (threat system), obsess over others' perceptions (social cognition), and lose access to their values-based decision-making (executive control).

The neuroscience of approval-seeking is different in neurodivergent brains. Differences in brain structure and function, especially in regions involved in social reward, emotion and self-reflection, mean that neurodivergent individuals may experience, seek or respond to approval in ways that are distinct from neurotypical individuals. As ever, being client-led and working with them to help them understand their thinking will provide the key to supporting neurodivergent thinking individuals.

Brain chemistry

Once again, the neurochemistry of approval-seeking involves three key systems working together to create behaviourally addictive patterns.

Dopamine drives anticipatory craving for validation, creating the same neurochemical signature as substance addiction.

Serotonin affects social hierarchy processing. When dysregulated, it can contribute to insecurity and a heightened need for validation, triggering clients to either desperately seek higher status through approval or accept lower status to avoid conflict.

Oxytocin, while promoting connection, in approval-dependent contexts, can reinforce emotional dependency on others' opinions for self-worth when social approval becomes the primary bonding mechanism.

Approval-seeking theory in action

Amir's story illustrates how approval-seeking can quietly trap achievers in careers that look successful on paper but feel hollow in practice. By focusing on his own words and fears, we can see how several major theories help explain the patterns that held him back.

"I love to achieve... but during my degree, I just couldn't find the drive"

Amir's admission highlights the gap between what he was expected to pursue and what actually motivated him:

- **Bandura's Social Learning and Social Cognitive Theory** explains how Amir internalised the model of success visible in his family: prestigious degrees and high-status careers. He observed that compliance with these expectations brought approval, while noncompliance risked shame.

- **Kelman's Social Influence Theory** further clarifies this pattern. Amir's choice of engineering complied with parental and cultural expectations, reinforced by his identification with admired figures like his mother. However, the absence of genuine internalisation left him drained and unmotivated.
- **Self-Determination Theory (Deci and Ryan)** helps us understand why: his autonomy was constrained, competence was undermined by lack of interest, and relatedness felt conditional. The absence of these three psychological nutrients created a lack of motivation, leaving him disengaged despite external achievements.

"My 2:2 felt like a failure... I feel like I'm failing them again"

This belief shows how academic outcomes were entangled with cultural and familial approval:

- **Young's Schema Theory** identifies an Approval-Seeking schema reinforced by Failure and Defectiveness/Shame schemas. Amir's degree result became proof of inadequacy, shaping his belief that he was letting his parents down.
- **Bowlby's Attachment Theory (later expanded by Ainsworth)** suggests an anxious attachment pattern: approval equated with love, leaving Amir hypersensitive to perceived disappointment. Academic performance became a proxy for emotional connection.
- **Deci and Ryan's Self-Determination Theory** again explains the erosion of competence. Because Amir could not connect effort to authentic mastery, his degree outcome deepened self-doubt and reinforced external dependency for validation.

"What I hadn't fully voiced was the deeper fear - the fear of being a disappointment"

At the heart of Amir's struggle lay the terror of losing his parents' pride:

- **Attachment Theory** shows how conditional approval threatened his relationship security. Amir avoided risks or authentic choices to protect potentially fragile family bonds.
- **Kelman's Social Influence Theory** highlights the compliance that came from fearing disapproval more than failure. Amir's paralysis was a way to avoid triggering rejection.
- **Schema Theory** points to enmeshment, where Amir's identity was not yet distinct from his parents' expectations. His self-concept felt incomplete without their approval, reinforcing the fear that individuality might equal abandonment.

"I am worried that I will never find what is right for me and may never actually achieve my potential"

This anxiety reveals how approval-seeking distorts confidence and stifles self-efficacy:

- **Bandura's Social Learning Theory** explains how Amir's repeated exposure to one approved path (i.e. engineering, finance, status careers) weakened his sense of agency in pursuing alternatives. His self-efficacy faltered as he doubted his capacity to succeed outside those models.
- **Schema Theory** again highlights how defectiveness and failure beliefs limited his imagination, creating paralysis rather than experimentation.
- **Self-Determination Theory** shows how a prolonged lack of autonomy and conditional relatedness produces amotivation. Without the safety to try, Amir feared he would never fulfil his potential.

What Amir's story shows us

Amir's words reveal how approval-seeking takes hold when love, pride and worth feel conditional on performance. *"I love to achieve... but I couldn't find the drive"* highlights how his compliance without internalisation drains motivation. *"My 2:2 felt like a failure... I feel like I'm failing them again"* shows how schemas and anxious attachment distort self-worth, turning results into emotional verdicts. *"The deeper fear – the fear of being a disappointment"* uncovers the relational cost of approval-seeking, where autonomy feels too risky. Finally, *"I am worried I will never find what is right for me"* reflects how diminished self-efficacy and amotivation stall progress and obscure potential.

Taken together, Amir's words show three insights:

- **Approval-seeking thrives where autonomy is suppressed** and performance is overvalued.
- **Conditional love and cultural expectations fuel schemas** and attachment anxieties, making self-worth fragile.
- **Sustainable growth requires restoring autonomy, competence and relatedness**, so approval becomes an outcome of authentic action, not its driver.

In the next section, we will explore how coaching helped Amir reduce his reliance on external validation, build confidence in his own judgement, and act from values rather than approval.

Decoding and resolving Amir's approval-seeking tendencies

Our early coaching conversations centred on giving Amir space to reflect and recalibrate. We explored his personality, skills and reasons for choosing engineering for his university degree. It quickly became clear his decision reflected his parents' desire for him to have a respected, secure career. When we explored what he wanted, Amir identified values around creativity and developing something new. Although present in engineering, none of his courses appealed, apart from a mild interest in product design. Even then, something was missing. I asked him to define what creativity meant to him and give an example. He described cooking meals from whatever ingredients he could find as his happy place, where he felt free, creative and in flow. We explored why this kind of creativity resonated more than engineering. "Because it's how we connect and share food and news from our day," he said. That sense of bonding was what had been missing. When I asked why this mattered so much, he replied, "It's part of my culture – coming together over food and enjoying special moments." His family always appreciated his cooking. This helped us return to the idea of a career that served him rather than just his parents.

We explored the tensions between autonomy and approval, and the quiet pressure born of love and hope. I asked him what he thought I would want for my own adult children. "To be happy, healthy, and independent," he replied. When I asked if he thought that's what his parents wanted for him too, his face lit up. The question opened the door to a different future. I encouraged him to try a new strategy with his parents. Rather than keeping them at arm's length, could he show them an alternative path that still led to success and stability and ask them to help him? Amir chose to be brave and told his mother he wanted to combine the product development skills from his degree with his passion for food. Priya embraced it, and they researched roles together. Through her network, she was able to introduce him to someone at a confectionery manufacturer who offered Amir a short placement to test the idea. He loved it. Because of it, he was able to secure a two-month placement developing spiced olive mixes and mezes, taking them from concept to packaging. "It's amazing," he said. "It's like the product development modules at uni, but now I care about what I'm creating." As soon as the context became meaningful, his motivation returned. For the first time in years, Amir felt purposeful. Each step grew his confidence and autonomy.

In our sessions, we reframed each supposed wrong turn as redirection. Amir realised that his engineering degree had not been a waste of time. Instead, it gave him the development mindset he needed as a food development chef. His earlier engineering placements were not detours but lessons in resilience and professionalism. His 2:2 wasn't a failure – it reflected misalignment and not inadequacy. Perhaps the biggest shift came in his relationship with his parents. Priya, who had been part of the journey, could now see the difference. "He's more focused and motivated than ever before," she said to me in an email. "What a great start."

Amir had not abandoned his family's dreams. He had reinterpreted them, using his skills in a meaningful context. Doing so meant that he had been able to build a version of success that honoured both his heritage and individuality. The goal he set in our session, to become a product development chef, was coming to life. He no longer felt the need to seek permission. He was building something real that he could own, share and take pride in. Amir is now working full-time as a product development chef in an artisan food company. His career is no longer something he's trying to escape. Instead, it is something he is actively and proudly building.

*****

Using the ABCDE model to help Amir move forward

Activating event

His mother had initiated coaching out of concern that he was not making progress towards a professional career. Though he had completed several relevant placements, Amir felt unmotivated, confused and afraid of disappointing his high-achieving parents.

Beliefs

Amir held several unhelpful hidden beliefs which were holding him back, including:

- *"If I don't pursue engineering, I'll be letting my parents down."*

- *"My 2:2 means I'm not good enough."*

- *"If I fail to meet their expectations, they'll be ashamed or disappointed in me."*

- *"Being creative only counts if it fits the traditional idea of success."*

Together, these had created a sense of being stuck in non-graduate work and a creeping sense of futility.

Underlying these beliefs were cultural and familial expectations, and a deep-seated fear that choosing authenticity over approval would result in rejection by the people who mattered most to him. This melange of beliefs set against a sense that there was something else better for him created some significant cognitive dissonance and distortion which needed to be resolved. The stress of this was evident in his flat tone and overall subdued body language.

Consequences

These beliefs led to several consequences we needed to address in our sessions together:

Emotional consequences

Amir was experiencing an increasing sense of anxiety and guilt, combined with a deep fear of letting his parents down, which was adversely affecting his self-confidence and autonomy.

Behavioural consequences

He found himself in career paralysis, taking refuge in avoidance through familiar, unthreatening, if unfulfilling barista work that kept him safely below the radar of expectations.

Cognitive consequences

The more time passed after graduation, the more his thinking narrowed. He was struggling to see a way forward and felt trapped in an internal conflict between wanting meaningful work and his desperate need to please his parents.

Dispute

Through coaching, I gently challenged Amir to examine his beliefs and develop his autonomy through several key interventions:

Questioning deeper parental motivations

This opened Amir to the possibility that his parents' surface expectations might mask deeper, more flexible hopes.

Reframing the parent-child dynamic

Rather than keeping his parents at arm's length or seeing them as judges, we explored how to make them allies, which resulted in transforming the power dynamic from pressured to collaborative.

Discovering authentic values

Exploring what made cooking meaningful to him uncovered his core values of creativity, community and connection – values that could be honoured in a career context.

Reframing past experiences

Seeing his degree outcome not as failure but as misalignment enabled him to see that his engineering background was not wasted time but rather highly valuable preparation for product development in a field he cared about.

Addressing the fear directly

Exploring his fear of losing approval helped him to understand what was actually preventing him from achieving the very success his parents wanted for him. It helped him to realise that authentic achievement in an area he loved would bring more genuine pride than forced success in engineering.

Effect

By exploring what he valued – creativity, community and contribution – Amir began to see a different future. He developed a stronger sense of autonomy through more empowering beliefs and perspectives. He reframed his relationship with his parents, recognising that involving them could create connection rather than conflict. He saw that the most significant outcome of his degree was not the grade, but the product development skillset and mindset he had cultivated. Most importantly, Amir realised he could create a career he was proud of on his own terms and one that reflected his cultural context, honoured his individuality and still made his parents proud.

Activities to create changes in approval-seeking thinking and behaviour

Long-term approval-seeking undermines self-esteem, mental health, authentic relationships and personal growth. Breaking this cycle means that as practitioners we need to help clients to improve their internal validation, work within those boundaries and build self-awareness and self-compassion. The activities that follow use journalling to help clients with strong approval-seeking tendencies to mitigate their impact enabling them to experience genuine personal and professional fulfilment and success on their terms. The activities can be used either on their own or as a sequence of three.

ACTIVITY 1: IDENTIFYING YOUR BRAIN INFLUENCERS: RECOGNISING EXTERNAL VOICES IN CAREER DECISION-MAKING

In an increasingly noisy world, it can be hard to make sense of the myriad of options and conflicting voices and opinions we encounter daily. As a result, our sense of self represented by our inner voice can become drowned out. When this happens, it becomes harder for us to make authentic decisions that reflect our true selves and desires, particularly where approval-seeking is at play.

This activity is designed to help clients surface and challenge approval-driven beliefs and shift towards autonomy by identifying the influence of others' voices on their thinking, whether parents, teachers, significant others, friends, managers or society at large.. The activity helps clients to identify internalised negative beliefs based on others' "should imperatives" (e.g. *"My father said...,"* *"At school, I was told...,"* *"My line manager expects..."*) and change these to intrinsically authentic beliefs and choices so they can move forward confidently.

The activity uses a neuroscience-informed approach to surface unhelpful thinking by asking clients coaching and journalling questions. This uses the brain's reticular activating system (RAS) to heighten awareness of specific thought patterns, helping clients make more conscious choices. The RAS acts as a filtering mechanism that determines what information from our environment, including our internal thoughts, enters our conscious awareness. As an example of your RAS in action, consider how after buying a new car, you suddenly start noticing that same model everywhere. The car was something that was always there, but previously filtered out of your awareness. By priming clients to notice "should" statements in the activity, the RAS becomes sensitised to these patterns, making previously unconscious approval-seeking thoughts more visible in daily life.

To enable your client to notice unhelpful thinking and begin to tune back into their authentic self and voice, start by asking them to list five to seven recurring thoughts or self-imposed "shoulds" and "musts" (e.g. *"I should be in a graduate/senior role by now," "I must prove myself"*).

For each "should," ask the client to identify:

* *"Whose voice is this?"*
* *"Where did this belief come from?"*
* *"Is it still serving you – or limiting you?"*
* *"Does this fuel your definition of success and happiness or frustrate it?"*

Then, invite them to rewrite each "should" as an "I choose" statement based on their values.

For example, *"I choose to grow at my own pace so I can lead with integrity."*

This approach supports a powerful shift from "should" to "I choose" language, which helps clients reclaim ownership of their career decisions and build confidence in their authentic voice. Once this work has begun in a coaching session, clients benefit most by using it as a follow-on journalling activity, which the coach and client can then discuss and build on in subsequent sessions. For best results, it is worth encouraging your client to journal for one to two weeks between sessions to allow the RAS to identify patterns in real-world contexts fully. The extended observation period ensures that insights emerge naturally from real-world experiences, leading to lasting change rather than superficial awareness.

ACTIVITY 2: ESCAPING THE APPROVAL TRAP: NEGATING THE POWER OF INFLUENCERS

Approval-seeking becomes particularly problematic when it operates unconsciously, shaping our decisions and behaviours without our awareness. Many achievers find themselves caught in subtle approval traps which cause them to automatically adjust their choices, opinions and career paths to gain validation from others. These patterns often remain invisible until we systematically examine how approval-seeking manifests across different areas of our lives.

This reflective audit activity is designed to help clients gain conscious awareness of their approval-seeking patterns in action and understand the hidden costs of these behaviours. By carrying out a comprehensive mapping exercise, clients develop the ability to identify where they are compromising authenticity for acceptance, so they can begin making more intentional choices about when seeking approval serves them versus when it limits their potential.

The activity works by making unconscious patterns visible through systematic analysis supported by journalling. When clients see the full scope of their approval-seeking behaviours alongside their emotional, mental and professional costs, they develop both the motivation and awareness needed to experiment with more authentic approaches. This activity can be used alongside the Identifying Your Brain Influencers activity or as a standalone exercise for clients already aware of their external influencers.

To begin the activity, ask the client to draw a three-column table with these headings:

1. "*Whom do I seek approval from?*"

2. "*How do I try to gain their approval?*"

3. "*What is the cost to me (emotionally, mentally, professionally)?*"

Then guide your client to consider a range of different contexts: workplace relationships, family dynamics, social circles and professional networks, helping them to make connections between common behavioural patterns across those different contexts. If you are working with a client who is likely to feel a sense of overwhelm if they uncover too many patterns at once, you may want to use a version of this where the focus is solely on one relationship or context first. Remember to encourage self-compassion as clients work through this activity with you, particularly if you notice a sense of shame or guilt in their reactions when they realise the extent to which they people-please, for instance. Using a normalising comment such as, "This behaviour that once served to keep you safe is now keeping you stuck" acts to mitigate those feelings and also to signal that change is both desirable and possible.

Once the initial audit is complete, encourage reflection using these prompts:

- "*What are you compromising to maintain this approval?*"
- "*Where could you test a new behaviour rooted in authenticity rather than fear?*"

Encouraging your client to undertake some further journalling between sessions will help them gain deeper insights, particularly of buried patterns. The following journal prompts that align with the three columns will help with this:

1. *"Whose disapproval do I fear most in my professional life?"*

2. *"What do I say 'yes' to that I'd rather say 'no' to?"*

3. *"Where do I feel resentful or exhausted after interactions?"*

In the next session, you can assist your client in identifying patterns and developing strategies to change their behaviour and thinking towards approval using questions like:

- *"Which approval-seeking behaviours feel most automatic or unconscious?"*
- *"Where might you experiment with small, authentic responses?"*

This systematic approach transforms abstract approval-seeking patterns into concrete, actionable insights. The extended journalling period between sessions once again helps clients gain greater clarity about the true cost of external approval-seeking, enabling them to open up to and begin redirecting their need for validation from external sources towards developing their own sense of intrinsic worth and authenticity.

ACTIVITY 3: ACHIEVING AUTHENTICALLY: VALUES-ALIGNED ACTION

The previous two activities focus on identifying and mapping approval-seeking patterns, creating awareness of how external validation drives decision-making. However, awareness alone is insufficient for lasting change. Clients need to actively rebuild their capacity for internal validation, learning to recognise and celebrate actions that align with their authentic values, regardless of others' reactions or recognition.

This tracking activity is designed to help clients shift from dependence on external validation to intrinsic motivation by systematically noticing and recording value-aligned actions, thereby creating new neural pathways. Many approval-seekers have become so accustomed to measuring success through others' responses that they have lost touch with their own internal compass and voice. By deliberately tracking authentic actions and the feelings they generate, clients begin rebuilding neural pathways that support self-determined behaviour and internal satisfaction. When clients consistently notice and acknowledge their own value-aligned choices, they strengthen their capacity for self-validation while gradually reducing dependence on external approval. This process gently disrupts the approval-feedback loop that keeps clients trapped in reactive, people-pleasing patterns. It can be used alone, as a follow-on to the previous two activities and as a follow-on activity to the Life Values Compass exercise from Chapter 2.

In this activity, the Achieving Authentically tracking process involves daily journalling for 7–14 days. To help the client feel confident about undertaking this task, as well as explaining what they will need to do, it may be helpful to work through an example with them beforehand.

The activity uses the following specific prompts to help clients notice and develop confidence in authentic action:

- *"What did I do today that aligned with my values, even if no one saw or praised it?"*
- *"What action did I take today that was brave or authentic, even if it was not perfect?"*
- *"How did I feel about that?"*

Encourage your client to notice small, everyday actions rather than searching for dramatic gestures. Examples might include speaking up in a meeting or seminar despite knowing it might create tension, choosing to leave work on time to honour work-life balance, or declining a social invitation that felt draining. The focus should be on the internal satisfaction generated by authentic choices, not on achieving perfect outcomes or others' approval.

For clients who may be resistant to change and likely to quit during the first few days of journalling, it is helpful to frame the activity which encourages them to keep going, even if they feel some discomfort as they gain insights. If you are working with clients who are particularly highly approval-driven, then encouraging them to send you two or three written or recorded journal entries every week will help them to stay with the task without slipping back into validation-seeking behaviour.

During your debrief session with your client, look for patterns of growing intrinsic satisfaction and autonomy. Help your client notice how authentic actions generate different feelings than approval-seeking behaviours. These feelings are often characterised by a sense of calm confidence, peaceful alignment or quiet satisfaction rather than the temporary high of external validation.

This systematic approach to rebuilding internal validation creates sustainable change by training the brain to recognise and value authentic choices. The extended tracking period allows clients to experience the genuine satisfaction that comes from self-determined action, gradually reducing their dependence on external validation while building confidence in their own judgement and values.

Taken together, these three activities enable clients to identify external influences, use them to map approval patterns and then rebuild internal validation. The progression creates a complete reflection-led coaching journey from awareness to sustainable change.

Summary

While a natural part of being human, approval-seeking becomes a thief when it overrides authenticity and self-worth. When clients depend on external validation to feel safe, successful or accepted, they often sacrifice their values, strengths and talents, struggle to make autonomous choices, and overextend themselves. By helping them recognise and shift these patterns, they can develop more fully and confidently because of an enhanced sense of their intrinsic motivation. Left unchecked, approval-seeking can be detrimental to clients as they take on too much to stay liked, needed or impressive. Those who persist in using approval-seeking habits and behaviour can find themselves falling victim to the fourth of our Seven Career Thieves, the Thief of Overwhelm, the topic of the next chapter.

3. The Thief of Approval-Seeking
At a glance

Working definition: "The habitual tendency to seek validation, acceptance, or recognition from others, often at the expense of one's own needs, values, or authenticity, to gain reassurance, avoid disapproval, or maintain social harmony."

Key theories and models:

1. **Social Influence Theory (Kelman, 1958):** Behaviour shifts through compliance, identification or internalisation, showing how people adapt to gain approval or avoid rejection.
2. **Attachment Theory (Bowlby, 1969):** Insecure attachment styles shape adult approval-seeking, with anxious patterns fuelling people-pleasing and fear of rejection.
3. **Social Cognitive (SCT) and Social Learning Theory (SLT) (Bandura, 1977/1986):** Approval-seeking is learnt through observing rewarded behaviours, imitation and reinforcement, linking external praise to safety and belonging.

Impact and context:

Undermines decision-making, innovation and leadership; increases burnout and overperformance.

Women seek approval more in social/relationship settings; men in success/recognition contexts.

High in hierarchical sectors (finance, law, consulting); customer-facing roles (sales, hospitality).

Neurodivergent individuals can show intense approval-seeking due to social experiences.

- **Early career:** Heavy reliance on validation.
- **Mid-career:** More strategic.
- **Late career:** Reduced as authenticity is prioritised.

Warning signs:

- **Fear of disappointing:** "If I don't meet expectations, I'll let people down."
- **Fear of rejection:** "If I'm authentic, people might not accept me."
- **Fear of conflict:** "If I disagree, I'll damage relationships."
- **Fear of being ordinary:** "If I'm not impressive, I'll be forgotten."
- **Fear of losing love:** "My worth depends on making others proud."
- **Fear of standing out:** "If I'm different, I won't belong."
- **Fear of making wrong choices:** "Others know better than I do what's right."

Acting to please others

4. **Self-Determination Theory (Deci and Ryan, 1985):** Autonomy, competence and relatedness underpin motivation. Unmet needs increase reliance on external validation over authenticity.
5. **Schema Theory (Young, 1990s):** Unmet childhood needs create maladaptive approval-seeking schemas, where validation is prioritised over authentic choices.
6. **Social Cognitive Theory:** Self-efficacy beliefs are weakened when validation depends on others rather than personal mastery and authentic achievement.

Neuroscience:

Social rewards activate the same brain circuits as primary survival needs, explaining why approval feels essential:

- **Reward system:** Treats social validation as a survival need, flooding with dopamine.
- **Threat detection:** Interprets potential disapproval as genuine danger.
- **Social cognition:** Hyperactive scanning and predicting others' responses.
- **Executive control:** Compromised authentic decision-making and boundary-setting.

Neurochemistry creates addictive patterns where dopamine, serotonin and oxytocin fluctuations reinforce approval-dependent behaviour.

Key coaching activities:

1. **Identifying Brain Influencers:** Recognise external voices in career decision-making and transform "should" statements into "I choose" language.
2. **Escaping the Approval Trap:** Map approval-seeking patterns across relationships to help understand their emotional and professional costs.
3. **Achieving Authentically:** Build internal validation through tracking values-aligned actions and celebrating authentic choices.

Core takeaway: Shift from **external validation** to **internal compass**.

4| The Thief of Overwhelm

Where demand consistently exceeds capacity

"You can do anything - but not everything."
David Allen, executive coach, author and productivity specialist.

Charlie's story

By the time Charlie reached out for support, she felt like she was constantly running to keep up and failing. The pattern of becoming overwhelmed had been quietly developing for years, not helped by her perfectionist tendencies. Once a naturally curious and technically gifted professional, Charlie now felt mentally foggy, emotionally stressed and perpetually preoccupied. "Right now, I'm lost on which step to do next," she told me, "It's not like something that has happened all of a sudden – it's a build-up." She clearly felt mentally overloaded, and buried continually under the weight of too many competing demands.

Her previous role in a 24/7 manufacturing company involved maintaining and optimising complex systems, which were often ones that nobody else fully understood. Over time, she had become the go-to person for thorny technical issues, with an internal reputation for solving problems that others found too difficult. But that reputation came at a cost. "People just assumed I'd handle it," she said. "Because I always have."

That was the problem. The more Charlie proved herself, the more invisible she became. With no support team and limited managerial oversight, she carried critical system knowledge on her own. There were no back-ups, no shared responsibility and no room to step away. "If something went wrong, there was no one else. And if it failed, it would all come back to me."

This sense of sole accountability kept Charlie in a state of constant mental load, anticipating what might go wrong, replaying old fixes and worrying about unseen risks. There were not often moments of high drama, but there was a continual, quiet, relentless sense of strain. Even outside work, she found it hard to switch off. "There was always something running in my head. A what-if. A check. A loop."

The constant worry was beginning to affect her sleep, leaving her feeling tired and anxious most days. She had not experienced a major failure, but that only seemed to raise the stakes. Her perfectionism meant everything had to be right the first time. Any mistake felt catastrophic in her mind, even if in reality, that was not true. She was caught in a cycle of over-preparation, over-functioning and cognitive overload, which constantly left her feeling overwhelmed and unprepared. While she was exceptionally good at her job, she was beginning to lose the sense of enjoyment she used to experience. She was beginning to think that it was no longer sustainable. So, rationalising that the problem was related to the environment she was working in, she decided to move to another company.

His new job, again in manufacturing, had been meant to offer a fresh start. However, it did not take long for her sense of overwhelm to return. Once again, she found herself feeling overextended and still saying yes to everything. And once again, her focus and motivation were fading. "I wasn't in crisis. But I knew I couldn't keep doing things the same way." That was when she opted for some coaching.

*****

So, what is overwhelm?

Although there is no one formal definition of overwhelm, based on psychological and theoretical sources, overwhelm can be defined as a psychological state where one feels wholly submerged by thoughts and emotions about current or perceived problems, characterised by cognitive overload, emotional dysregulation and behavioural paralysis when demands exceed one's perceived capacity to manage effectively. Cognitive overload happens where there is too much information to process. In this context, our ability to self-regulate and make thoughtful, ethical choices can be undermined.

From a **personality perspective** using OCEAN as a lens, research consistently shows that personality plays a significant role in how individuals experience and manage overwhelm. People high in **Neuroticism** are significantly more prone to overwhelm due to emotional reactivity, negative stress mindsets and maladaptive coping strategies like rumination. In contrast, those high in **Conscientiousness** tend to be more resilient, organised and flexible in their responses to pressure. Traits such as **Extraversion**, **Agreeableness** and **Openness** offer some protection by promoting adaptive coping, social support-seeking and creative stress management.

While personality shapes how individuals react to pressure, motivation determines what drives their behaviour under stress. Overwhelm is particularly common among those with high achievement motivation (nAch), especially when perfectionism or fear of failure distorts their goals. Intrinsically motivated individuals tend to be more resilient. In contrast, those driven by external validation or avoidance, such as a need for approval or a fear of making mistakes, are more vulnerable to overload. Research also shows that low autonomy and lack of perceived control significantly increase the risk of chronic overwhelm, highlighting the importance of aligning motivation with meaningful, self-directed goals (see later in this chapter for more on Self-Determination Theory).

Why should we be worried about overwhelm?

Overwhelm is a double-edged experience. It is harmful when prolonged or unmanaged, but potentially motivating when short-lived and well-supported. Its harmful effects are well documented: cognitive functioning can decline, making it harder to concentrate, make decisions or retain information. Emotionally, it often leads to anxiety, irritability, exhaustion and, in more serious cases, depression, especially among those high in neuroticism or perfectionism. Physically, sustained overwhelm increases risks such as poor sleep, fatigue, gastrointestinal problems and even cardiovascular issues. Behaviourally, it can trigger withdrawal, procrastination and reduced performance at work or in study, with knock-on effects on relationships and team dynamics.

However, not all overwhelm is damaging. In manageable amounts, it can prompt individuals to reassess priorities, streamline commitments and seek support or new coping strategies. For some, it serves as a wake-up call, encouraging growth, assertiveness and setting boundaries. It may even spark bursts of innovation, problem-solving or productivity, particularly in conscientious individuals with strong support systems.

In the **workplace**, overwhelm is a silent issue that can lead to a decline in individual performance, a reduction in collaboration and innovation, declining morale, poor client services and the breakdown of team dynamics. It is often mistaken for disengagement or disorganisation in an individual, but it is usually merely a sign of an employee trying to manage competing tasks without clear priorities. This "silent overload" can lead to reactive decision-making, breakdowns in collaboration and a decline in innovation. Overwhelmed staff can over-function or fail to delegate, creating bottlenecks and a culture of constant urgency. As pressure increases, people may opt out through disengagement, sick leave or resignation. To address overwhelm in the workplace, proactive organisations need to ensure high value is placed on psychological safety, prioritisation and sustainable productivity, where asking for support or saying no is seen as good judgement.

In **education**, overwhelm is also prevalent, affecting both students and staff. It tends to emerge from a combination of excessive academic pressure, lack of clarity and limited support. Students are often expected to juggle heavy workloads, tight deadlines, high-stakes assessments and competing commitments, all while navigating uncertainty about grades, expectations prospects and purpose. These pressures can lead to cognitive overload, emotional exhaustion and, over time, disengagement from learning altogether.

Transitions, such as moving from school to university or starting new programmes, are particularly risky periods. In these moments, students are adapting to unfamiliar systems, expectations and environments, often without the scaffolded support they need. At the same time, staff and educators face their own sources of overwhelm, including increased administrative demands, lack of autonomy, reduced support and the emotional toll of supporting struggling learners. This can result in reduced creativity, diminished teaching quality and higher levels of burnout and turnover, which undermine the wider learning environment.

When students and staff are emotionally stretched, collaboration weakens, innovation stalls and wellbeing declines. Several factors have been found to buffer against this: psychological safety in classrooms, access to mental health support, training in coping and time management strategies and strong peer relationships. Conversely, overwhelm is more likely to escalate in settings where fear of failure, perfectionism and a lack of control dominate. As in the workplace, the solution lies not only in managing workload but in building sustainable, supportive systems that protect wellbeing while enabling growth.

When it comes to **age**, the impact of overwhelm varies across different age groups. It is a common issue among young adults, particularly those in their late teens, 20s and early 30s, who are more likely to experience stress. Older adults are generally significantly less likely to report overwhelm and are more resilient psychologically. This is due to improved emotional wellbeing, a greater emphasis on positive experiences and support networks, although they take longer to recover physically from episodes of acute stress. It is important to note that chronic stressors, such as health challenges or caregiving responsibilities, can still lead to overwhelm in later life, however. The age-overwhelm correlation can be explained by life experience and coping strategies, as well as emotional regulation. However, chronic or severe stress can affect individuals of any age, especially if protective factors are absent.

Gender is a strong predictor of overwhelm, with women consistently reporting higher levels of stress and emotional exhaustion than men across cultures and age groups. This disparity is especially pronounced during the prime working years, when many women juggle multiple roles, including career, caregiving and domestic responsibilities, leading to chronic role overload, as in Charlie's case. Societal expectations, workplace inequities and lower perceived support further exacerbate their experience of overwhelm. Women are more likely to internalise stress and use emotion-focused coping strategies, while men often underreport overwhelm or express it through avoidance or externalising behaviours. These differences contribute to higher rates of anxiety, depression and burnout among women, especially when intersectional factors like single parenthood, economic insecurity or discrimination are present.

Neurodivergent individuals are significantly more prone to overwhelm than their neurotypical peers, due to differences in sensory processing, emotional regulation and executive functioning. Sensory overload, difficulty managing multiple tasks and challenges with time management often result in a heightened, persistent sense of mental strain. For many, overwhelm can trigger shutdowns, emotional meltdowns or contribute to long-term burnout. Environments such as open offices, unpredictable classrooms and unclear expectations further intensify this experience. Higher stress reactivity, emotional rumination and difficulties identifying feelings (e.g. alexithymia, a personality trait characterised by difficulty identifying, processing and describing emotions, both in oneself and others) compound the issue.

Individuals with lower **socio-economic status** (SES) experience significantly higher levels of overwhelm and chronic stress due to increased exposure to persistent stressors, such as financial insecurity, unstable housing, and limited access to support, and fewer coping resources. This imbalance contributes to elevated rates of anxiety, depression and emotional overload, particularly among children, adolescents and young adults from low-income backgrounds. Mechanisms such as a reduced sense of control, chronic threat perception and limited access to healthcare or support systems further intensify feelings of overwhelm. In contrast, higher SES provides greater buffering through access to resources, support networks and a stronger sense of agency. These patterns contribute to long-term disparities in wellbeing and mental health, reinforcing the need for structural interventions that reduce inequality and promote resilience.

Culture and ethnicity also play a vital role in shaping how overwhelm is experienced, expressed and coped with. Cultural norms influence everything from emotional expression to beliefs about control, responsibility and the mind-body connection. For instance, some cultures describe overwhelm through specific syndromes, such as *khyâl* attacks in Cambodia, *taijin kyofusho* in Japan or *ataques de nervios* in Latin communities, highlighting culturally embedded understandings of distress. Ethnic minority groups, especially in Western societies, often face added burdens in the form of discrimination, acculturative stress and reduced access to mental health resources. This "double stress," accumulated from the demands of daily life and minority-specific challenges, leads to higher levels of chronic overwhelm, especially in immigrant, Black, Latino and Native American populations. In a UK context, British South Asian and Black British communities often experience additional stressors related to racism, intergenerational expectations and stigma around mental health. Cultural norms around emotional restraint and family honour can make it harder to talk openly about distress, leading to underreporting and delayed support-seeking. At the same time, strong religious or community networks can act as protective factors, buffering the impact of overwhelm. An individual's cultural background also influences coping abilities. Collectivist cultures tend to emphasise group harmony and suppress individual distress, which may reduce outward signs of overwhelm but delay support-seeking. In contrast, individualist cultures encourage emotional disclosure and autonomy, often leading to earlier identification of stress, but also higher reported rates. A strong sense of cultural identity, community belonging and supportive family structures can buffer overwhelm, while identity conflict, isolation and social exclusion intensify it.

Overwhelm and sectors

While overwhelm is a universal phenomenon in all sectors, its prevalence, causes and consequences vary significantly due to differing demands, organisational structures and cultural expectations. Specific fields, particularly health and social care, education, finance, professional services, defence and blue light services, consistently report the highest rates of overwhelm and work-related stress. The nature of the sector shapes motivations and triggers for overwhelm:

- **High-intensity sectors** such as **healthcare, education, policing, law, finance** and **consulting** experience elevated overwhelm due to workload pressure, emotional labour and low autonomy, often without matching reward or recognition.
- **Fast-paced and tech-driven sectors** like **telecoms, media** and **IT** face overwhelm from constant change, digital overload, continuous innovation and around-the-clock availability.
- **Sales-driven environments** such as **property** and **retail** generate overwhelm through fluctuating targets, unpredictable schedules and limited job control.
- **Collaborative or structured sectors**, including **production management** and **related technical roles**, and **sports/fitness professions**, report lower overwhelm, likely due to clearer job expectations, greater autonomy and healthier workplace climates.

Across all sectors, overwhelm is intensified by low psychological safety, poor recovery time and imbalances between demand and support, making sector-sensitive strategies essential for effective intervention. Sectors with greater autonomy, strong peer cultures and clear organisational structures tend to report lower stress levels.

When it comes to **entrepreneurs**, chronic overwhelm significantly impairs entrepreneurial risk-taking, innovation and overall business success. As cognitive and emotional resources are depleted, overwhelmed entrepreneurs tend to avoid risks, make erratic decisions or miss promising opportunities. Creativity suffers due to mental overload, which reduces experimentation and stifles innovation. Wellbeing declines, resulting in diminished focus, resilience and the ability to bounce back from setbacks. However, positive emotional states, restorative activities like leisure, crafting and supportive environments that encourage learning and experimentation can help mitigate these effects. Managing overwhelm is crucial to sustaining entrepreneurial risk-taking, creative capacity and long-term venture success.

Overwhelm across the career lifespan

Overwhelm experiences vary with career stages, influenced by responsibilities, expectations and life circumstances. Understanding these patterns helps tailor support and intervention more effectively.

Early careers: Young professionals and achievers often experience high levels of uncertainty, financial instability and pressure to prove themselves. This stage is marked by imposter syndrome, perfectionism and a tendency to overcommit, leading to anxiety, self-doubt and chronic stress. With limited experience and few boundaries, early-career professionals are particularly vulnerable to burnout.

Mid-careers: By this stage, individuals often find themselves juggling increased workplace responsibilities, typically managerial or specialist roles, alongside complex personal commitments such as childcare or eldercare. Overwhelm frequently stems from accumulated roles, habitual overworking and a drive to continue progressing without shedding past duties. Without conscious boundary-setting, this phase can lead to emotional exhaustion and declining fulfilment.

Late careers and retirement: At this point, overwhelm tends to shift from workload pressure to emotional and existential themes. Concerns about retirement, loss of identity and connections and legacy can surface, alongside changes in energy and priorities. While this stage can trigger reflection and uncertainty, including finance-related issues, many older professionals draw on greater resilience and established coping strategies, helping them navigate the transition more easily.

The neuroscience of overwhelm

Overwhelm is not simply mental fatigue; it's a whole-brain event that disrupts multiple interconnected brain systems simultaneously, creating the performance and learning challenges seen in both education and the workplace. The **prefrontal cortex**, the brain's executive centre responsible for planning, decision-making and working memory, becomes overloaded and less effective at managing competing workplace demands. This explains why high-performing employees suddenly struggle with tasks they previously handled efficiently.

Meanwhile, the **amygdala**, the brain's threat detection system, remains hyperactive, interpreting work pressures as genuine threats and flooding the brain with stress signals. The **anterior cingulate cortex**, which usually helps filter important information from workplace noise, becomes less discriminating, making employees feel like "everything is urgent." This creates a neurological cascade where emotional reactivity increases while cognitive control decreases – the exact opposite of what's needed for effective learning and performance.

These overlapping processes explain why overwhelmed clients often feel emotionally reactive, cognitively foggy and physically drained. Overwhelm also strains the brain's executive functions, which manage working memory, task-switching and self-control. As these systems become saturated, professionals experience mental "lock-up," forgetfulness and decision paralysis. Support cells in the brain, called astrocytes, play a role in managing this process by calming overstimulated neurons, thereby helping to restore balance once the threat has passed.

When in a state of overwhelm, several sensory and cognitive processing changes take place. The brain shifts focus inward. Sensory input is dampened, narrowing attention in a tunnel-vision effect that increases rumination and negative thought loops. Contrary to the idea that overwhelm is caused by too much sensory information, neuroscience suggests that certain sensory regions shut down, contributing to a feeling of cognitive disconnection and reduced responsiveness.

This internal overload also taxes the brain's limited energy resources. The brain consumes around 20% of the body's energy at rest, and high-demand thinking under stress can quickly deplete this reserve. As energy levels decline, so does the ability to regulate emotions, concentrate or maintain self-control, deepening the experience of overwhelm.

The Zeigarnik Effect also offers a helpful explanation for why sustained overwhelm happens. It states that the brain struggles to "let go" of incomplete tasks or unresolved commitments. These mental "open loops" consume working memory and attention, keeping the brain in a heightened state of arousal, even when actual task volume is low. Think of it as having too many tabs open on your computer at the same time, and your hard drive constantly spinning. Without closure, it will eventually become unresponsive.

Brain chemistry

At the neurochemical level, overwhelm is driven by surges in cortisol and noradrenaline. While these chemicals enhance alertness in short bursts, chronic exposure depletes mental energy and contributes to emotional exhaustion. Noradrenaline also initially heightens arousal but also triggers astrocyte responses that eventually support neural recovery.

Neurodivergent individuals experience overwhelm differently due to distinct neurological patterns. They often have heightened sensory sensitivity and reduced filtering of external stimuli, leading to rapid cognitive overload. Emotionally, their reactions may be more intense due to altered communication between the **amygdala** and **prefrontal cortex**, making emotional regulation more difficult. Executive function challenges, such as difficulties with planning, task-switching and prioritising, further increase susceptibility to overwhelm.

Neuroimaging reveals reduced or disrupted connectivity between emotional and regulatory brain centres, as well as overconnectivity in other regions, which can heighten internal "noise" and stress responses. These neurological differences can manifest as shutdowns or emotional meltdowns, leading to chronic fatigue, even in the absence of objectively heavy workloads. Despite these challenges, neurodivergent individuals often exhibit unique strengths in areas such as creativity, pattern recognition and detailed thinking. Supporting them effectively means creating tailored environments and strategies that reflect their distinct cognitive wiring.

Whether working with neurotypical or neurodivergent individuals, brain-based understanding explains common overwhelm behaviours where people who are usually decisive fail to make simple choices, those who prefer working with detail start missing deadlines, and typically friendly and communicative individuals begin to become more irritable and withdrawn. These are not character flaws or motivation issues but rather predictable neurological responses to cognitive overload that can be addressed with targeted interventions.

Interventions that reduce cortisol, support recovery and restore prefrontal activation are essential for helping individuals regain clarity, calm and control.

Overwhelm theory in action

Charlie's story illustrates how overwhelm creeps in gradually, eroding clarity and confidence until everyday work feels unsustainable. By anchoring theory through her own words, we can see how multiple theories and models together explain the cycle of overload, responsibility and strain that she experienced.

"Right now, I'm kind of lost on which step to do next"

Charlie described feeling paralysed by competing demands:

- **Lazarus and Folkman's Stress Appraisal and Coping Theory** explains this reaction. Her primary appraisal framed her workload as threatening and with too much riding on her role, while her secondary appraisal judged her coping resources as inadequate, given the lack of team or managerial support.

This appraisal dynamic helps us see why she felt foggy and unable to decide on next steps: overwhelm is less about the objective situation than the perceived imbalance between demands and resources.

"People just assumed I'd handle it - because I always have."

Charlie's competence became her trap:

- **Kahn, French, Caplan, van Harrison et al.'s Person-Environment Fit Theory** reveals a demands-abilities misfit: the organisation relied excessively on her skills without supplying support, backup or shared responsibility.
- **Karasek et al.'s Job Demands-Resources Model** highlights how high technical and time demands, combined with a lack of resources, drained her energy and motivation.

These theories and models show how a valued strength, in this case being the reliable problem-solver, became a liability when boundaries were absent, leaving her invisible and overloaded.

"There was always something running in my head. A what-if. A check. A loop"

Charlie's description captures the mental toll of overwhelm:

- **Sweller's Cognitive Load Theory** explains this as working memory saturation. Her role carried high intrinsic load (complex systems she alone understood), compounded by extraneous load (isolation, lack of clarity, constant vigilance).

- **The Zeigarnik Effect** helps explain why tasks lingered: unresolved problems and "open loops" consumed her mental bandwidth, keeping her in a state of rumination even outside work.

Together, these perspectives show why she experienced ongoing mental noise and reduced capacity to focus, innovate or rest.

"If something went wrong, there was no one else. And if it failed, it would all come back to me"

This statement shows how sole accountability intensified Charlie's sense of being under strain:

- **Karasek's Demand-Control-Support Model** identifies Charlie's role as a classic high-strain job, characterised by relentless demands, minimal autonomy in task management and little social support.
- Even after moving jobs, the pattern repeated, because the structural imbalance of demands versus control/support remained.

This highlights why overwhelm persisted despite changing roles. Unless the balance of demand, control and support shifts, the same cycle reappears.

"I wasn't in crisis. But I knew I couldn't keep doing things the same way"

These words mark Charlie's turning point, reflecting the recognition that overwhelm had become unsustainable. It shows the moment when reappraisal and coaching intervention became possible.

What Charlie's story shows us

Charlie's experience demonstrates how overwhelm accumulates quietly through over-responsibility, blurred boundaries and persistent imbalance between demands and resources. *"I'm lost on which step to do next"* reveals how appraisal processes turn pressure into paralysis. *"People just assumed I'd handle it"* highlights how reliability without support erodes wellbeing. *"There was always something running in my head"* illustrates the cognitive overload of unclosed loops. Finally, *"If something went wrong... it would all come back to me"* shows the cost of high demand, low support and minimal control.

Together, these insights reveal three key points:

- **Overwhelm thrives** when appraisal frames multiple demands as threats and resources as inadequate.
- **Strengths can become liabilities** when organisations over-rely on them without support or boundaries.
- **Chronic overload undermines cognitive clarity and wellbeing,** but recovery begins when clients learn to rebalance demand, control and support.

In the next section, we will explore how coaching helped Charlie step back from automatic over-responsibility, restore clarity and build strategies for sustainable contribution.

Decoding and resolving Charlie's overwhelm tendencies

In our work together, Charlie began to unpick the stories going round in her head. We examined the underlying beliefs fuelling her over-responsibility: perfectionism, fear of failure and a narrative about being the one who always had to hold things together. From there, we reframed these patterns not as flaws, but as misplaced strength, her natural qualities that needed better boundaries, not abandonment.

Step by step, Charlie built the skills and confidence to pause before saying yes. We worked through the step-by-step Five Ds productivity strategy I had developed earlier to help clients triage and manage competing priorities. I knew that using it with Charlie would help her create a strategy for reducing overload and increasing her level of work satisfaction.

We started off by helping her to **Decide** what she really wanted to do based on what matters most to her in her work and where she felt she could add the most value. That meant that this second step was to **Delete/Declutter** what was not necessary on her to-do list. She recognised that she also needed to make some changes to her physical work environment so she could be more productive too. For her third step, she needed to learn to **Delegate/Deflect** where appropriate to someone better placed to help based on her evaluation from the previous two steps. Step four was to **Delay** what did not need to be done immediately by scheduling it for later, by which time, it may not even need doing. The final step after running the previous stages was simply to **Do** what was left. Finally, Charlie began to feel a sense of hope that her workload could become manageable.

One of Charlie's biggest wins lay in developing her ability to say no. Rather than simply declining work, with encouragement to test it out, Charlie learnt how to redirect diplomatically. Instead of saying "I'm too busy," which she worried would make her sound defensive and unhelpful, she practised new scripts which helped her develop better boundaries such as *"That's something I'd normally support with, but based on current priorities, I think [person X] is better placed to help right now,"* and *"I'm currently at full capacity. To take this on and maintain quality, I'd need to drop something else. Which would you prefer me to prioritise?"*

To Charlie's surprise, these responses were well received. "People accepted it. I was worried they'd push back, but no one did. It gave me space to think again."

As the cognitive load lifted, so did her clarity. Using the Five D process helped Charlie reconnect with what she most enjoyed – and what she no longer wanted to do. Technical challenges still mattered to her, but she no longer wanted to work under continual conditions of urgency and isolation. She wanted to work in teams, contribute to meaningful outcomes and have time for deep focus rather than constant interruption.

One of the most significant mindset shifts was recognising that she did not have to be the heroine. Helping people did not have to mean doing everything – or constantly sacrificing herself in the process. "I'm still someone who likes to help," she reflected. "But now I check by asking myself, 'Am I really the right person for this? Or am I just stepping in by default?'"

She began exploring crafting a new career direction within the same organisation so that she could honour her favourite skills, preserve her energy and build on her track record. Together, we explored roles in risk management, quality assurance and cybersecurity as potential areas where her analytical mindset and attention to detail would be valued, and she would not feel totally overwhelmed.

"I used to think I had to say yes to be useful," she told me. "Now I know that the real value comes when I say yes to the right things – and no to the rest."

Charlie's journey is a powerful reminder that overwhelm doesn't always look dramatic. Sometimes it creeps in quietly, through over-responsibility and blurred boundaries. When we work with clients who are willing to reflect and reset, they can come back to a place of clarity, purpose and calm.

*****

Using the ABCDE model to help Charlie move forward

Activating event
Charlie had become increasingly overwhelmed in her previous and current roles, despite moving jobs. In both roles, she found herself overextended. She had a pattern of carrying too much responsibility, saying yes to too many tasks, and being constantly on alert for what might go wrong. The return of a heightened sense of cognitive and emotional overload shortly after moving into a new job caused her to realise something important. As she said herself: "I can't keep doing things the same way."

Beliefs

Charlie's internal beliefs were shaped by perfectionism, over-responsibility and fear of failure. These showed up during our sessions as:

- *"If I don't do it, no one else will – and something will go wrong."*

- *"Saying no means I'm letting people down."*

- *"Being a good colleague means always being helpful, even if I'm overloaded."*

- *"My worth is tied to being the one who can fix everything."*

- *"If I'm not constantly available, I'll be replaced or seen as less valuable."*

These beliefs drove her to ignore her own limits and default to saying yes, leading to continuous overwhelm through scarcity thinking and people-pleasing tendencies.

Consequences

As a result of these beliefs, Charlie experienced several unhelpful elements:

- **Emotional stress** driven by too many demands, too quickly, left her feeling increasingly anxious.

- **Cognitive overload** led to difficulty focusing, a constant mental loop of "what ifs," and diminished clarity.

- **Behavioural patterns** which caused her to over-prepare, take on others' work, avoid delegation and fail to protect her own time and attention.

Despite changing jobs, the same patterns followed her, highlighting how internal beliefs, rather than simply external environments, were driving her continual sense of overload.

Dispute

Through coaching, Charlie began exploring some Socratic coaching questions I asked her about the most important of her ingrained beliefs including:

- *"Is it really true that you are the only one who can do this well?"*

- *"Could saying no actually help others grow or make space for better solutions?"*

- *"What happens if you pause before saying yes? Could you respond more wisely?"*

- *"Does being helpful mean doing everything, or choosing where you add the most value?"*

By challenging these assumptions and testing out new approaches, Charlie started to shift her mindset from automatic over-functioning to considered contribution.

Effect

As a result, Charlie adopted more supportive and sustainable beliefs, including the following:

- *"I'm more effective when I focus on the right things, not everything."*

- *"Saying no, or redirecting, can be a form of professional responsibility."*

- *"My strengths, like problem-solving and risk awareness, need structure and boundaries to thrive."*

- *"I can be a valued team member without doing it all myself."*

- *"Clarity and calm are better measures of contribution than constant availability."*

Armed with these beliefs, Charlie gained confidence in setting boundaries, applying the Five Ds framework and exploring career paths within the same organisation that allowed her to use her strengths without becoming overloaded or overwhelmed.

It is worth noting that the Five Ds framework could be extended to become a Six D framework, where the final D stands for **Develop** in the sense of helping others grow, an important addition to include when coaching, particularly managers who are new to the role. (I am grateful to Claire Johnson for this addition.)

Activities to create changes in overwhelm thinking and behaviour

As we have seen in Charlie's case, chronic overwhelm can erode clarity, confidence and the capacity for sustainable achievement. It often stems not just from external demands, but from internalised beliefs around responsibility, control and self-worth. As practitioners, we can support clients by helping them restore a sense of agency, reduce cognitive load and build realistic, self-aligned strategies for managing pressure. The following reflective activities are designed to help overwhelmed clients pause, reprioritise and reset. They can be used individually or in sequence to support insight, behaviour change and long-term wellbeing.

ACTIVITY 1: UNDERSTANDING YOUR INTERNAL REVS

Overwhelm rarely appears out of nowhere. Instead, it builds gradually as mental demands increase, and the brain shifts from a calm focus into a reactive survival mode. In the 1990s, neuroscientist and stress researcher, Bruce McEwen, developed the groundbreaking concept of *allostatic load* – the cumulative "wear and tear" that occurs when the body's stress systems are repeatedly activated without adequate recovery. McEwen demonstrated that stress responses involve a biological cascade where initial adaptive responses (like cortisol and adrenaline release) become harmful when chronically activated, causing emotional reactivity to increase while cognitive control decreases.

Just as a car's rev counter helps drivers avoid engine damage by monitoring performance under pressure, this activity uses the same principle to help clients recognise their own mental and emotional "RPM" or "revolutions per minute" zones. Understanding these zones enables earlier intervention to prevent clients from reaching the neurological redline. By learning to recognise their rising mental RPMs, clients can make proactive adjustments before they hit total overwhelm. Operating in the warning and overwhelm zones can create lasting physiological damage, while staying in the optimal zone enables proper recovery and resilience. Understanding this helps practitioners emphasise to clients that recognising early warning signs is not just about immediate performance – it is about preventing the long-term health consequences of chronic stress activation.

Using the rev counter as a metaphor with clients helps them consider how their brain operates and recognise that it works best when running within the optimal range and neither too slow nor too fast. When life gets intense, their ability to recognise when their mental RPMs start rising enables them to notice when they are pushing too hard and reset before hitting the red line.

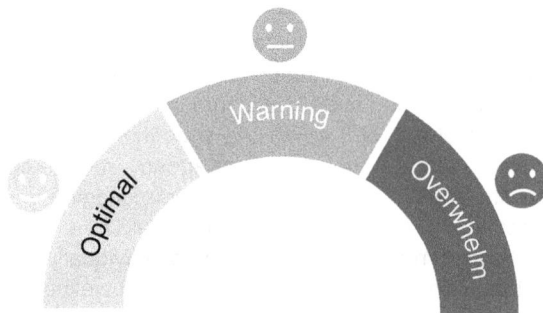

Encourage your client to draw a rev counter gauge and mark three zones: the optimal zone on the left, the warning zone in the middle and the overwhelm zone on the right. Now explore each zone in turn with your client, encouraging them to capture what they discover in words, drawings or emojis in each zone:

- **For the optimal zone,** invite them to describe how they feel **mentally** (e.g. clear thinking), **emotionally** (e.g. calm, confident) and **behaviourally** (e.g. proactive, collaborative) when they're at their best. Ask them to note any bodily sensations that signal balance.
- **For the warning zone,** ask what subtle signs emerge as pressure builds, whether **thoughts, feelings** or **behaviours**. Invite them to consider what others have observed in them when in this phase and help them to explore their early "running hot" indicators, including physical cues.
- **For the overwhelm zone,** help them articulate what full overwhelm looks and feels like and encourage them to consider what happens to their clarity, decisions, behaviour and relationships. Again, explore physical sensations or reactions (e.g. shallow breathing, tension, irritability).

Note: some neurodivergent clients may struggle to identify internal states, so you may need to offer specific examples to help them identify their own, for example "In the optimal zone, you may find that when you get started on time, you can focus for 30 minutes," "In the warning zone, you may find that you start re-reading the same sentence over and over," and "In the overwhelm zone, your brain shuts down and you can't decide what to do next."

Next, encourage your client to become more aware of triggers and how they can shift back to a more optimal zone by exploring reflective questions such as:

- *"Where are your RPMs running right now?"*
- *"What warning signs have you been ignoring recently?"*
- *"What typically helps you shift back into the optimal zone?"*

Encourage them to check in with their revs frequently, by asking themselves, "How am I feeling right now?"

Going through this process enables clients to see overwhelm not as a crisis but as a predictable progression they can learn to manage.

When clients clearly understand their personal rev patterns, they become less reactive to pressure and more strategic about managing their mental resources. They can recognise the quiet signals that precede overwhelm and develop personalised strategies for staying in their optimal zone.

The visual nature of the rev counter makes it a memorable tool they can reference long after your session ends, and perfect as a daily or weekly journalling activity if that approach works for them.

ACTIVITY 2: REFRAMING OVERWHELM: A PERSPECTIVE RESET

When clients are overwhelmed, it is often not just because of external demands, but because of how they interpret those demands internally. Lazarus and Folkman's Stress Appraisal and Coping Theory, that we looked at earlier, reminds us that it is our appraisal of a situation, how threatening or unmanageable it feels, that activates stress responses, not the situation itself. This activity uses this theory to provide a structured approach that helps clients reframe overwhelming thoughts and regain a sense of agency and perspective.

This exercise is particularly effective for clients caught in catastrophising, perfectionistic or emotionally reactive thinking loops. It can also be used to follow up the Rev Counter activity, especially when clients identify themselves in the warning or overwhelm zones and provides a way to help them recode how they perceive threats and challenges.

Using it when clients are caught in cognitive overload caused by distorted interpretations of pressure is particularly effective. It provides them with a repeatable internal process for reality-checking their fears, recognising their capacity and aligning their responses with their values.

When working with neurodivergent clients, you may need to make some adaptations. Some clients may find it challenging to identify their internal "threat narratives" or articulate emotional responses. If a client struggles with this, offer concrete examples, such as "My boss will think I'm incompetent" or "Everyone will judge me," and consider using emotion rating scales (1–10) or body-based indicators instead of abstract emotional language. You can also break the reframing process into smaller steps, working through one reframe technique at a time rather than offering multiple options simultaneously.

Stage 1: Primary appraisal: Spotting the threat narrative

In this first stage, your aim is to encourage your client to describe a current situation that feels overwhelming. These types of questions are helpful for this:

- *"What's the story your brain is telling you about this situation?"*
- *"What do you fear might happen if this doesn't go well?"*

The following questions will help you to explore how they are currently interpreting the situation:

- *"Is it being appraised as a threat (something dangerous, overwhelming, or high stakes)?"*

"Is a challenge (difficult but manageable)?"

"Or as neutral (something that just needs doing)?"

This is the moment to look together with your client for signs of three common cognitive distortions:

Catastrophising: That is, imagining worst-case scenarios from minor setbacks, for example:

"If I'm late to this meeting, I'll lose my job."

"This headache must be a brain tumour."

"My presentation wasn't perfect – my career's over."

Watch for: Language like *disaster*, *ruined* or *terrible*, and physical anxiety about minor issues.

Black-and-white thinking: That is, seeing things in extremes with no middle ground, such as:

"One mistake means the whole report or essay is worthless."

"I didn't get the promotion, so I've failed completely."

Watch for: Absolute terms like *always*, *never*, *all*, or *nothing*, and all-or-nothing reactions.

Future-tripping: This is worrying about imagined future problems instead of focusing on the present, such as:

"What if the economy crashes and I lose everything?"

"What if my child struggles next year at school?"

"What if AI makes my job obsolete?"

Look for: Repetitive "what-if" thinking, decisions based on distant hypotheticals, or constant scanning for future threats.

By helping the client name these patterns, they can start to gain distance from them.

Stage 2: Secondary appraisal: Resource reality check

Next, invite your client to map out what support they actually have. Ask them to create two columns titled:

- **Column A: "Resources I have"**: This covers skills, previous experience, strengths, natural abilities, tools, people, time, inner resilience, and
- **Column B: "Resources I think I need (and why)"**: This helps clients to realise that they have overestimated what is required or are discounting resources they already possess.

At this point, it is helpful to ask clarifying questions like:

"What's worked for you in a similar situation before?"

"Who or what could support you that you haven't yet considered?"

At this point, clients often feel less anxious because the process has helped them to surface strengths they had overlooked under pressure.

Stage 3: Reappraisal practice: Shifting the lens

Now that the original appraisal and available resources are visible, it is a great moment to encourage your client to actively reframe the situation using any of the following prompts:

- **Evidence-based thinking**: "What evidence do I have for and against my original belief?"
- **Resource-focused reframe**: "Given what I now see I have, how could I approach this differently?"
- **Perspective-taking**: "If someone I respect were in this situation, how might they handle it?"
- **Values-aligned thinking**: "What choice here would best reflect my core values and long-term goals?"

These reframes help the client shift from threat-based thinking to more constructive, empowered responses.

To enable the client to reflect on what has changed and consolidate what they have learnt from the process, here are some helpful follow-up reflection questions:

- *"How has your emotional response shifted through this process?"*
- *"What feels possible now that didn't before?"*
- *"What approach/reframe do you want to return to when this pattern shows up again?"*
- *"How could you remind yourself to use this process in the moment?"*

You might suggest they create a short "overwhelm reframe checklist" to revisit during future pressure points. You can also use these questions together with others as journalling prompts for them to use to consolidate their pattern awareness and new approaches in their thinking and behaviours.

ACTIVITY 3: CLOSING THE TABS: A MENTAL DECLUTTERING ACTIVITY

This activity builds on the Five Ds and the previous exercises. It also works well as a standalone intervention. Closing the Tabs provides a scaffolded exercise to help clients to identify and reduce unnecessary mental burden using a familiar technology metaphor. This intervention directly addresses the Zeigarnik Effect, where the brain struggles to "let go" of incomplete tasks. By systematically identifying and categorising these "open tabs," clients can reduce the working memory burden that keeps their brain running at maximum capacity, even when actual task volume seems manageable. The activity also uses Sweller's three categories of *intrinsic load* (the core tasks that require genuine mental effort and cannot be simplified), *extraneous load* (mental burden from poor organisation, unclear instructions, distractions), and *germane or growth load* (learning-related processing that builds understanding/skills) as a lens to help clients prioritise tabs better over time.

Introduce the activity to your client by explaining that just as having too many browser tabs open slows down your computer and drains its processing power, having too many mental "tabs" running creates cognitive overload and mental sluggishness. If you are working with a client who is showing signs of overwhelm at the start of the task, you might suggest that they take a breath and slow their breathing down before they start. (Also, see Chapter 7 for how to use grounding breaths.)

When working with neurodivergent clients, remember to check whether the categorisation process in this activity feels overwhelming. This may be particularly the case for those with executive function differences or perfectionist tendencies. If sorting feels too demanding, encourage clients to focus on just one category at a time with breaks between each section. It is helpful to remind them there is no "wrong" way to categorise items – if they change their mind about where something belongs, that is completely normal. For clients who prefer visual structure, consider writing the three categories (Essential, Extraneous, Learning) on separate pieces of paper as physical reminders during the sorting process. You can use paper and Post-it notes, whiteboards or a digital whiteboard if coaching remotely.

Step 1: The brain dump

Ask your client to draw a big plus sign to create four boxes, one for each of the following:

- **Work/academic tabs:** Projects, deadlines, meetings, assignments,
- **Personal responsibility tabs:** Errands, appointments, family obligations,

- **Unfinished business tabs:** Incomplete conversations, pending decisions, "someday" items, and
- **Background worry tabs:** Things they're mentally tracking or ruminating about.

Now, encourage your client to review each box with you, helping them to identify and write down all the mental "tabs" currently running in their mind in each of the four boxes.

Step 2: Sorting the tab load

Now, ask your client to return to their original four categories (work/academic, personal responsibilities, unfinished business, background worries). For each category, help them sort the items into three types of mental load by either colour-coding, numbering or creating a separate set of columns or sub-boxes.

Then, introduce the following three subcategories:

- **Essential tabs:** These are the tasks that genuinely matter right now and require mental effort that you can't delegate or delay. Examples include *"preparing for a team presentation,"* *"booking a doctor's appointment"* or *"supporting a family member today."*
- **Extraneous/cluttering tabs:** These are items that take up space in your brain but don't add value or could be streamlined. They often stem from poor organisation, unclear expectations or distractions. Examples include: *"wondering if I should reorganise my notes,"* *"feeling guilty about not replying to every message,"* or *"worrying about something I can't control."*
- **Learning tabs:** These are tabs that reflect a growth mindset, that is, the mental effort a client is putting into skill-building or development. They are valuable but need intentional pacing. Examples include: *"taking an online course,"* *"practising using a new piece of software"* or *"reading about a new approach at work."*

Here are some questions to explore with your client as you go through each area:

- *"Is this tab essential to handle right now?"*
- *"Is it clutter you could close, clarify, or set aside?"*
- *"Is it something you are learning from that needs structure and time?"*
- *"What system(s) could you create to maintain lower cognitive load over time?"*
- *"What do you notice about how you feel when you change your approach on this?"*

As you work with your client, encourage them to cross out, reframe or schedule items where possible. The aim here is not just to tidy the list, but to lighten the cognitive load and improve mental clarity.

Doing so will also help the client to establish better systems and practices. Using tools like an online to-do list or physical planning tool such as a Bullet Journal may help with this.

Step 3: Managing the tab load

This step focuses on supporting your client to develop closing or optimising strategies for each tab, for instance:

- **For essential tabs**: Break complex tasks into smaller chunks, schedule focused time blocks, keep only what you are actively working on "open,"
- **For extraneous/background clutter tabs**: Close unnecessary tabs immediately, bookmark important items for later, eliminate mental distractions, clarify expectations and create external memory systems, and
- **Learning tabs**: Prioritise high-value learning, schedule dedicated development time, connect new skills to existing knowledge, focus on learning that reduces future mental load.

Here are some helpful reflection questions you could use to encourage a change of approach, to identify next steps towards change and anchoring better habits and behaviours:

- *"How many mental tabs do you typically have running at once?"*
- *"Which background clutter tabs could you close immediately?"*
- *"What would it feel like to run with fewer mental tabs open?"*
- *"How could you prevent accumulating so many tabs in future?"*

For clients who need to uncover unhelpful patterns and strategies over a longer period, again journalling can be helpful to help them declutter mentally so they can be more productive and effective without the emotional and psychological wear and tear.

Summary

As we have seen in Charlie's story, while overwhelm can occasionally serve as a motivating force, it becomes a thief when demands consistently exceed our perceived capacity to cope, creating a cascade of cognitive, emotional and physical consequences. When clients become trapped in patterns of over-responsibility, perfectionist thinking and poor boundary management, they sacrifice clarity, confidence and sustainable performance. Neuroscience reveals that chronic overwhelm can create lasting physiological damage through repeated stress activation. At the same time, psychological theories demonstrate that our appraisal of situations, rather than the actual situations themselves, often drives overwhelming responses. Left unchecked, overwhelm erodes mental resources, depletes emotional reserves and undermines the capacity for meaningful achievement. Those who persist in overwhelming patterns often find themselves falling victim to the fifth of our Seven Thieves, the Thief of Depletion, the topic of the next chapter.

4. The Thief of Overwhelm
At a glance

Working definition: "A psychological state where one feels wholly submerged by thoughts and emotions about current or perceived problems, characterised by cognitive overload, emotional dysregulation, and behavioural paralysis when demands exceed one's perceived capacity to manage effectively."

Key theories and models:

1. **Stress Appraisal and Coping Theory (Lazarus and Folkman, 1984):** Overwhelm arises from how individuals interpret demands and evaluate their coping resources, shaped by perceived threat and available support.
2. **Cognitive Load Theory (Sweller, 1988):** Overwhelm occurs when information or mental effort exceeds working memory capacity through intrinsic, extraneous and germane loads.
3. **Person-Environment Fit Theory (University of Michigan, 1970s):** Overwhelm results from a mismatch between a person's abilities/needs and environmental demands/resources, particularly as subjectively perceived.

Impact and context:

Often mistaken for disengagement when actually trying to manage competing demands without priorities.

Young adults (teens–30s) most affected; women report higher stress due to multiple roles.

Neurodivergent individuals can be significantly more prone due to sensory/executive function differences.

High in healthcare, education, finance, consulting; "always-on" digital culture increases risk.

- **Early career:** Uncertainty and proving oneself.
- **Mid-career:** Accumulated responsibilities.
- **Late career:** Identity transitions.

Warning signs:

- **Mental fog and confusion**: "I'm lost on which step to do next."
- **Decision paralysis:** Simple choices become impossible to make.
- **Racing thoughts:** Constant "what-if" loops and rumination.
- **Emotional exhaustion:** Feeling drained despite not doing much.
- **Physical tension:** Sleep disturbances, headaches, muscle tension and stomach problems.
- **Social withdrawal:** Avoiding people and reducing collaboration.
- **Perfectionist paralysis:** Everything feels urgent and critical.

Where demand consistently exceeds capacity

4. **Demand-Control-Support Model (Karasek, 1979 and Theorell and Johnson 1908s):** Overwhelm peaks when high demands combine with low control and minimal support, making autonomy an essential buffer against stress.
5. **Job Demands-Resources Model (Demerouti and Bakker, 2001):** Overwhelm emerges when demands outweigh available resources, leading to exhaustion unless buffered by personal strengths and resilience.
6. **Zeigarnik Effect:** The brain struggles to "let go" of incomplete tasks, consuming working memory and attention, keeping the brain in a heightened arousal state.

Neuroscience:

Overwhelm is a whole-brain event disrupting multiple interconnected brain systems simultaneously:

- **Prefrontal cortex:** Executive overload reduces decision-making and working memory.
- **Amygdala:** Hyperactive threat detection floods brain with stress signals.
- **Anterior cingulate:** Less discriminating filtering makes everything feel urgent.
- **Astrocytes:** Support cells help calm overstimulated neurons during recovery.

The brain consumes 20% of the body's energy. High-demand thinking under stress quickly depletes reserves, reducing emotional regulation and self-control.

Key coaching activities:

1. **Understanding your Internal Revs:** Use the rev counter metaphor to recognise mental high rev zones and intervene before hitting neurological redline.
2. **Reframing Overwhelm:** Use stress appraisal theory to reality-check threat narratives and recognise available resources and capacity.
3. **Closing the Tabs:** Mental decluttering activity to identify and reduce unnecessary cognitive load using Zeigarnik Effect principles.

Core takeaway: Shift from **reactive overwhelm** to **proactive boundaries**.

5 | The Thief of Depletion

When the energy tanks are empty

> "Your energy is unique. Embrace it.
> Use it wisely. Make it count."
>
> Robin Sharma, lawyer-turned-leadership expert and author.

Ivan's story

When Ivan first reached out, he was not entirely sure what was wrong. On paper, he had everything going for him: a strong academic background in engineering and applied mathematics, fluency in multiple languages, a razor-sharp analytical mind and a deep commitment to succeeding professionally. But despite these strengths, he felt stuck. He'd completed his maths research master's successfully at one of the UK's top universities after years of focused study in Bulgaria and was now trying to get into a career in data science or consulting, where he could see there was opportunity. His visa clock was ticking, and the pressure to secure a job – almost any job – was mounting.

Ivan had already applied for more than forty positions. A few interviews had trickled in, but nothing had stuck. "I just feel... slow," he confessed in our first session. "Like I'm not progressing things the way I used to. Even reading job descriptions or application questions takes so much effort now."

His energy was low, but it wasn't burnout in the traditional sense. It was a more invisible depletion, that slow, cumulative exhaustion that builds when effort is constant and clarity is absent. Ivan was putting in tremendous effort every day to conform to the UK jobs market and system, but it was getting him nowhere and wearing him out. He was caught in a cycle of overdoing, second-guessing and questioning his path. Even decisions that once came easily, such as what jobs to apply for, and which interests to follow, now felt foggy and heavy, and he felt like he was wading through treacle.

It soon became clear that Ivan was living a pattern of depletion that kept quietly repeating itself, leaving him frustrated and angry.

Each time a new opportunity arose, whether in consulting, data science or energy modelling, he would dive in headfirst. He would research obsessively to minimise his risk of rejection, craft tailored applications, network strategically using LinkedIn and push himself hard to go above and beyond each time. And time after time, the result was the same: rejections, near misses or, worse still, being ghosted by recruiters. His non-UK profile, a tightening economy, and a surfeit of graduates all chasing a reducing number of opportunities was a challenging context to deal with for someone so used to working hard and achieving well. One particularly draining episode involved a multi-week case study for a promising analyst position that led nowhere. "It's like I keep sprinting down these paths," he said, "only to realise they're the wrong ones."

Each time that his energy would run out, he did what he had quietly learnt to do: he went home to Bulgaria to regroup. There, surrounded by family and the familiar conversations about their successful family manufacturing business, Ivan would rest and recover as he slipped back into familiar family rhythms. The contrast was stark. His parents and siblings were pragmatic, enterprising and full of momentum. Business decisions were made around the kitchen table. Ideas flowed. Progress happened. The environment did not feel heavy – it felt alive. And slowly, Ivan would begin to feel like himself again, ready to return to the UK, and try another route. Then the cycle would repeat itself.

He did not recognise himself in this pattern. And yet, it made sense. Ivan had pushed hard for years. He had considered a PhD but stopped short after realising that the heavy academic environment was draining rather than stimulating him. He described the final stages of his studies as cognitively overloading, leaving him "flattened" and unsure of what was next. The discipline that had once driven him was now fuelling indecision and perfectionism.

Our early work together focused on helping Ivan reconnect with who he was beyond his academic identity. He struggled initially to describe himself in three words. "Ambitious, disciplined… maybe smart?" he offered, half-joking. The words were technically accurate but emotionally hollow. They reflected what he *did*, not who he *was*. As we explored his values, Ivan admitted he had always seen his career as the highest priority. But something was shifting. "I still want to achieve," he said, "but I think I also want to enjoy life. I'm just not sure how to balance the two."

That tension between striving and thriving became the core of our work.

*****

So, what is depletion?

Although there is no single recognised definition, depletion can be explained as a gradual loss of mental, emotional or physical energy due to stress, effort or self-control. This makes it harder to concentrate, make decisions, maintain motivation or perform effectively at work or in learning environments. When an individual's personal resources are lowered, it often leads to poorer self-control, impulsivity and disengagement from tasks. When mental resources are low, this state is referred to as *ego depletion*. Researchers define ego depletion as: *"a state of diminished 'strength' or reduced resources that results from an initial act of self-control, which hampers subsequent self-control efforts."*

Those most susceptible to ego depletion tend to have high depletion sensitivity, low general trait self-control, high neuroticism, a strong belief that willpower is limited, high perceived fatigue, weaker motivation/ purpose state rather than action-oriented personalities and/or chronic stress. Chronic stress and emotional regulation also increase the risk of ego depletion due to constant demands on self-control resources. Understanding these agents can help tailor interventions for individuals at greater risk. The **Depletion Sensitivity Scale**, developed by Salmon et al., measures how prone an individual is to experiencing mental or emotional exhaustion in response to everyday effort or self-control demands, making it especially relevant in understanding vulnerability to stress, fatigue and burnout.

Depletion is a broader form of resource exhaustion that can occurs in all life domains, often preceding or occurring alongside burnout. It manifests as reduced motivation, mental fog, diminished resilience and a loss of energy or enthusiasm, especially in areas that once felt purposeful or rewarding. It often affects high-functioning individuals who continue to perform externally while feeling internally drained. High intrinsic motivation or a strong sense of autonomy can buffer against ego depletion.

From a personality perspective, personality traits strongly influence how individuals experience depletion. **Neuroticism** is the strongest predictor, increasing vulnerability to emotional exhaustion and burnout. **Conscientiousness** is protective but can slip under prolonged stress. **Extraversion** and **Agreeableness** also buffer against depletion, likely due to positive affect and social support. Finally, **Openness** has weaker effects but may support coping flexibility.

While personality traits influence how depletion is experienced, another important factor is **depletion sensitivity**, a tendency to feel drained more quickly than others. Individuals high in this trait burn through their mental and emotional energy faster, making them more vulnerable to exhaustion even in everyday situations. This highlights how **individual differences**, including personality, motivation and beliefs about self-control, shape not only how quickly depletion sets in, but how intensely it is felt. As self-regulation weakens during ego depletion, people may struggle to manage impulses or emotions, with anxiety, irritability or withdrawal becoming more likely. In fact, under severe depletion, even typically resilient individuals (such as the highly conscientious or emotionally stable) may temporarily behave more like those who are generally more reactive or impulsive, blurring the usual distinctions between personality types.

Why should we be worried about depletion?

This thief has a significant negative impact on personal wellbeing, work performance, relationships and long-term health. It directly lowers performance and engagement, weakens self-control and coping and reduces resilience to stress. Long-term depletion leads to burnout and health risks, as it increases the risk of anxiety, depression, cardiovascular problems and other health conditions. Depleted individuals are more irritable, impatient and less empathetic, damaging personal and professional relationships. They also lose social support, leading to further isolation and compounding exhaustion. Depletion also leads to productivity loss and workplace errors, as well as decreased innovation and adaptability. It signals deeper systemic issues, such as chronic overwork, lack of support, inadequate resources or unhealthy expectations.

In the **workplace**, employees who are "running on empty" may struggle with concentration, decision-making and motivation, leading to emotional and cognitive drain, irritability and reduced collaboration. This can lead to team breakdowns, lower morale, increased absenteeism and a decline in overall wellbeing. Recognising these signs early can help both employees and organisations recover and prevent deeper burnout. Psychological safety reduces the risk of depletion by allowing individuals to express concerns, admit mistakes and seek help without fear of judgement. In contrast, psychologically unsafe environments require constant vigilance and restraint, which can lead to chronic outcomes like burnout. Higher levels of psychological safety reduce emotional exhaustion and increase engagement, especially under pressure.

In **education**, depletion negatively impacts student performance, motivation and wellbeing, particularly in high-pressure academic settings. It leads to lower academic performance, decreased motivation, increased procrastination and errors. Emotional and behavioural outcomes include increased stress, burnout, anxiety and absenteeism. High demands and low resources increase the risk of depletion among students. Support and wellbeing programmes can help buffer students from depletion and promote resilience. Teachers and educators also suffer from depletion, as their teaching effectiveness declines due to overwork, stress or lack of resources. Chronic depletion is a risk factor for reduced educational attainment and higher dropout rates. Early experiences with academic depletion can shape attitudes towards learning, making future success more difficult. Depletion in education can be countered by a shift from pressure to purpose, creating environments that prioritise rest, reflection, autonomy and meaningful connection over relentless performance and output.

Age is a significant factor in the experience and expression of depletion, including mental, emotional and physical exhaustion, across different life stages. The connection between age and depletion is often U-shaped. Younger individuals are at higher risk due to inexperience and life transitions, while older adults face biological and social changes that can raise vulnerability. Those in their early career and young adulthood are at higher risk of emotional exhaustion and burnout, as individuals in these stages are learning to cope with demands and are more likely to experience depleted energy and emotional resources. Middle adulthood sees a decline in depletion, as people adapt to work requirements, increase skills, improve job fit and reduce family conflict. Later adulthood sees renewed vulnerability, particularly for women, due to biological ageing and new family responsibilities. Emotional regulation becomes stronger with age, and older adults may be more resistant to depletion effects due to greater life experience and emotion regulation. The impact of depletion can be mitigated by tailoring support for the different life stages, for instance, providing mentoring and coping strategies for younger adults, flexibility and work-life integration for midlife professionals, and health-conscious, purpose-driven engagement for older adults.

When it comes to **gender**, women are more likely to report higher levels of emotional exhaustion and burnout, especially in people-focused professions like healthcare, teaching and social work and over the age of 55. This difference is particularly evident in early and late career stages. Factors contributing to this include multiple roles and demands, workplace and societal expectations, and women's awareness of feelings of exhaustion. Men also experience depletion and burnout, but whereas women tend to report higher emotional exhaustion, men are more likely to express depletion as depersonalisation, that is, feeling detached or cynical about work. Life and career stages also play a role in depletion, with the gender gap narrowing in midlife. Supportive work environments, flexible arrangements, equal sharing of responsibilities at home and access to resources can help reduce gender disparities in depletion. Social support is particularly protective for women and enhances resilience for both genders.

Depletion in **neurodivergent individuals** is often intensified due to the constant cognitive, sensory and social effort required to navigate environments not designed with their needs in mind. Factors such as sensory overload, unclear expectations and rigid norms lead to faster draining energy and more frequent episodes of exhaustion. One key contributor is the effort of masking. The energy needed to consciously suppress or disguise neurodivergent traits to fit into neurotypical settings can be profoundly depleting over time. This sustained exertion can result in unique patterns of depletion, including increased sensory sensitivity, executive functioning difficulties, emotional dysregulation and even a loss of previously acquired skills. These symptoms are not always relieved by rest alone. Without appropriate accommodations and understanding, the risk of neurodivergent individuals facing severe, long-lasting depletion rises significantly. What may be neutral for neurotypical individuals can be highly demanding for neurodivergent people, making recognition, support and inclusive design essential to reducing depletion and enabling sustainable wellbeing and performance.

There is a strong negative correlation between **socio-economic status** (SES) and depletion, with individuals from lower-income backgrounds being more vulnerable to emotional exhaustion, cognitive fatigue and disengagement. This heightened risk stems from chronic financial stress, reduced autonomy, limited access to supportive resources and exposure to high-demand, low-control environments. In both educational and professional settings, lower SES is linked to higher rates of burnout, poorer mental health outcomes and greater difficulty recovering due to restricted access to healthcare and recovery spaces. These challenges often create a self-reinforcing cycle of stress and resource loss. However, protective factors such as personal resilience and targeted support interventions can buffer these effects and help reduce the impact of depletion in lower SES populations.

Across **cultures and ethnicities,** depletion is experienced and expressed differently according to values, coping norms and structural inequalities. In collectivist cultures, emotional restraint and a focus on group harmony may lead to suppressed stress and greater internal depletion, while more expressive cultures may externalise emotional exhaustion. Minority ethnic groups often face additional pressures, such as discrimination, masking or exclusion, that heighten the risk of emotional fatigue and disengagement, though underreporting and cultural stigma may obscure the data. While core symptoms of depletion (like emotional exhaustion and lowered motivation) are universal, their expression and severity vary across cultural contexts. Socio-economic disparities and systemic barriers compound risk for certain ethnic groups, particularly when support and inclusion are lacking. Recognising these cultural nuances is vital for developing equitable and effective approaches to addressing depletion in diverse educational, workplace and social environments.

Depletion and sectors

A universal challenge across sectors, depletion presents differently depending on the nature of the work, organisational culture and external pressures. While all industries experience some level of energy drain, certain roles and environments are particularly prone to chronic depletion due to intensity, unpredictability or emotional labour. Patterns of depletion vary by sector context:

- **High-intensity professional sectors** such as **finance**, **law** and **consulting** experience high levels of mental depletion due to long hours, relentless performance demands and high-stakes decision-making, often leading to emotional fatigue, reduced motivation and disengagement.
- **Public sector and education roles**, including **teaching, social care** and **local government,** report high depletion linked to resource scarcity, rising workloads and limited autonomy, which can lead to emotional exhaustion and feelings of ineffectiveness.

- **Healthcare and care professions** face persistent emotional and physical demands, exposure to trauma and staffing pressures, making them highly susceptible to compassion fatigue, decision fatigue and cumulative exhaustion.
- **Customer-facing industries** such as **retail**, **hospitality** and **leisure** see depletion driven by unpredictable hours, emotional labour and constant interpersonal demands, often resulting in irritability, absenteeism and reduced empathy.
- **Agriculture**, **construction** and **manufacturing** sectors experience significant physical depletion and stress due to long hours, safety risks and environmental or economic uncertainty, with limited access to support systems.
- **Creative and tech sectors** may experience more variable depletion, fluctuating between high engagement and overextension, particularly in roles with innovation pressure, "always-on" cultures, or output tied to identity.

Depletion is particularly prevalent among **entrepreneurs**, who face unique pressures that significantly heighten the risk of emotional, mental and physical exhaustion. Long hours, multiple responsibilities, decision fatigue and financial uncertainty combine with social isolation and identity strain to create a perfect storm for depletion. Studies show entrepreneurs report higher rates of burnout, anxiety and poor mental health than traditional employees, especially when lacking boundaries or support. While autonomy can offer protection, without proactive coping strategies, such as rest, connection and clear role separation, entrepreneurs are especially vulnerable to chronic depletion that undermines both wellbeing and long-term business success.

Depletion across the career lifespan

Depletion levels shift across the career lifespan, typically following a U-shaped pattern. It is highest in early and late career, and lowest during mid-career. Recognising these patterns enables individuals and organisations to provide timely, stage-specific support that sustains wellbeing and engagement throughout working life.

Early careers: These individuals are especially vulnerable due to inexperience, pressure to prove themselves and competing life transitions, often leading to emotional exhaustion.

Mid-careers: Here, individuals tend to experience greater stability, confidence and autonomy, which can buffer against depletion, though feelings of stagnation or overwhelming leadership duties may still pose risks.

Late careers and retirement: At this point, depletion may rise again due to physical decline, shifting priorities or caregiving demands, though some find renewed energy through mentoring or flexible work.

Recognising these patterns enables individuals and organisations to provide timely, stage-specific support that sustains wellbeing and engagement throughout working life.

Depletion significantly impacts career decision-making by lowering confidence, increasing indecision and steering individuals towards safer, less demanding paths that may not align with their true interests. Whether mentally or emotionally exhausted or both, people are less likely to explore options actively or make purposeful choices, often avoiding risk or challenge. Depletion can also prompt career shifts or withdrawal from misaligned roles, particularly when it turns into burnout and becomes unsustainable. Those with higher emotional intelligence and support systems are more resilient and able to make better-aligned decisions despite stress. Ultimately, depletion creates a negative feedback loop between career uncertainty and psychological strain, one that can be interrupted through rest, insight into personal patterns, guidance and skills for self-awareness so they can cope with and reduce depletion.

The neuroscience of depletion

Usually, the **prefrontal cortex** (PFC) helps regulate impulses and emotions through top-down control. However, with repeated mental or emotional exertion, this control can weaken, leading to lapses in self-regulation, increased impulsivity and emotional outbursts. During depletion, the **amygdala**, the brain's inbuilt threat alarm, becomes more reactive to negative or stressful stimuli, while connectivity between the PFC and the **amygdala** is reduced. As a result, we tend to react more strongly to negative events and find it harder to calm down. This combination is also a hallmark of anxiety, meaning depleted individuals may experience heightened worry, tension or a sense of threat, even in low-risk situations. The **anterior insula**, working with the PFC, monitors the perceived cost of effort, essentially tracking how much energy a task feels like it requires. Rather than simply "running out" of resources, the brain shifts into a protective state, recalibrating its motivation systems towards rest or avoidance. As perceived effort increases, the brain becomes more likely to disengage, making it easier to give in to temptations or distractions. This helps to explain why depleted individuals often feel more emotionally reactive, mentally unfocused and unmotivated, highlighting the importance of rest and recovery to restore self-regulation and emotional balance.

Brain chemistry

When someone is depleted, it is not just tiredness. Their brain chemistry shifts in ways that affect how they think, feel and act:

Glutamate, a neurotransmitter or chemical messenger that plays a crucial role in learning, memory, thinking and decision-making, accumulates in the **prefrontal cortex** as the brain becomes overstimulated and foggy. This makes it harder to focus, solve problems or manage emotions.

Dopamine levels drop. With lower amounts of the brain's reward and motivation chemical, motivation drops, making tasks feel harder and less satisfying.

Serotonin, which helps regulate mood, may also decline, making individuals more sensitive, irritable or low as their emotions feel bigger.

Cortisol, adrenaline and noradrenaline, the stress chemicals, all rise during periods of sustained effort or emotional pressure. While these stress chemicals help with short-term alertness and performance, when elevated for too long, they can impair focus, memory and emotional regulation, leaving individuals feeling wired, restless or easily overwhelmed. At the same time, stress-related inflammation in the brain (neuroinflammation) can develop, contributing to brain fog, low energy and mood problems.

Chronic stress and depletion can also reduce levels of **BDNF (Brain-Derived Neurotrophic Factor)**. This key protein supports neuroplasticity, the brain's ability to rewire and adapt over time, as well as emotional resilience and the brain's capacity to recover, learn and grow.

Depletion is not just about "feeling tired." It reflects a chemical and functional shift in the brain that makes it harder to think clearly, regulate emotions, stay motivated and recover. These changes are reversible with rest, recovery, supportive environments and practices that restore balance (e.g. sleep, movement, positive emotion and connection).

When working with **neurodivergent clients**, we need to recognise that while chronic stress disrupts brain chemistry and impairs emotional regulation in all brains, these effects can play out differently, and often more intensely, for neurodivergent individuals. Clients with autism, ADHD and other neurodivergent profiles are associated with natural variations in brain structure and function, including differences in connectivity, synaptic density and neurotransmitter systems. These differences can lead to heightened sensitivity to stress and unique patterns of energy use and recovery. As a result, demands that may cause temporary fatigue in neurotypical individuals can lead to deeper or longer-lasting exhaustion for those with neurodivergent profiles. Additional factors such as sensory overload, ongoing emotional regulation efforts and masking can further increase cognitive and emotional load. While the underlying mechanisms of stress and fatigue are shared, the experience of depletion in neurodivergent individuals is often shaped by these distinct neurological and social dynamics, calling for greater understanding and tailored support.

Depletion theory in action

Ivan's story shows how energy drains quietly over time until persistence turns into depletion. By anchoring his experience through his own words, we can see how five key theories together explain the slide from effort to exhaustion and the beginnings of recovery:

"I just feel... slow. Like I'm not progressing the way I used to"

Ivan's description of mental fog reflects the moment-to-moment cost of sustained effort.

- **Baumeister et al.'s Ego Depletion Theory** highlights how repeated acts of self-control and decision-making drained his limited self-regulatory capacity, leaving him fatigued and indecisive.
- **Hacker, Frese and Zapf's Action Regulation Theory (ART)** shows how the lack of clear goals and feedback forced him to operate at the most effortful knowledge-based level of regulation, increasing mental load and slowing his progress.

"It's like I keep sprinting down these paths only to realise they're the wrong ones"

Ivan captured the cycle of overinvestment and disappointment that left him exhausted.

- **Hobfoll's Conservation of Resources (COR) Theory** explains how heavy investment of time and energy without adequate returns created a downward spiral of loss, eroding Ivan's personal and emotional resources.
- **McEwen's Allostatic Load Theory** shows how these intense efforts repeatedly activated his body's stress systems. Without sufficient recovery, cumulative wear and tear built up, contributing to his fogginess and reduced resilience.

"Each time, I go home to Bulgaria to regroup"

Retreating to his family environment offered some respite, but the pattern of depletion resumed once he returned to the UK.

- **COR Theory** interprets these retreats as attempts to restore condition and energy resources through belonging and stability. Yet because the underlying effort-reward mismatch remained, recovery was only partial.
- **Action Regulation Theory (ART)** adds that breaks disrupted the immediate cycle but did not resolve the deeper misalignment between his tasks and strengths, so effortful regulation quickly resumed.
- **Allostatic Load Theory** suggests that rumination and persistent stress responses continued even in periods of rest, limiting the effectiveness of Ivan's regrouping efforts.

"Ambitious, disciplined... maybe smart?"

Ivan's identity became narrowed to performance, forcing him to sustain an image he no longer felt.

- **Hochschild and Grandey's Emotional Labour Theory** highlights how maintaining a façade of drive and competence while feeling exhausted creates emotional dissonance. This surface acting silently drained Ivan's energy and eroded his sense of his own authenticity.
- **COR Theory** shows how this identity strain threatened his resources, making his self-concept more fragile and vulnerable to depletion.

"I still want to achieve, but I also want to enjoy life"

This statement reflects a turning point, as Ivan recognised that persistence alone was not enough, and sustainability mattered as much.

- **Action Regulation Theory** points to the need for clearer goals, tasks aligned with his strengths and feedback systems that would allow him to move from effortful to more efficient regulation.
- **COR Theory** reframes his strategy around building gain spirals: investing in activities that replenish resources (such as AI and art) and restore self-efficacy.
- **Allostatic Load Theory** emphasises the need for rhythms of exertion and recovery to reduce the physiological cost of chronic stress.
- **Emotional Labour Theory** shows that moving towards environments where he could express himself genuinely, rather than projecting a false persona, was essential for recovery.

What Ivan's story shows us

Ivan's words reveal depletion as a gradual erosion of energy rather than sudden collapse. *"I feel... slow"* shows how sustained self-control and unstructured effort reduced clarity. *"I keep sprinting down wrong paths"* illustrates how repeated effort without reward leads to loss spirals and an accumulation of stress. *"I go home to regroup"* highlights a partial recovery that could not reset the underlying cycle. *"Ambitious, disciplined... maybe smart?"* reveals the cost of keeping identity tethered to performance. Finally, *"I want to achieve, but also enjoy life"* reframes success as sustainable progress, aligning goals and environments with authentic motivation.

Together, these patterns highlight the following three insights for us as practitioners:

- **Depletion builds in loops** such as overinvestment, poor returns and inadequate recovery, which compound over time.
- **Strengths and identity can become drains** when misaligned with values and context.

■ **Recovery begins with design changes** when clients focus on clarifying goals, creating gain spirals, supporting authenticity and embedding rhythms of effort and rest.

In the next section, we will explore how coaching helped Ivan recognise his depletion patterns, reconnect with energising activities and shift from draining persistence to sustainable, values-aligned progress.

Decoding and resolving Ivan's depletion tendencies

Through tools covered in earlier chapters, including the Life Values Compass and reflective journalling, Ivan had begun to notice how lopsided his energy had become. His efforts to get a job dominated, and connection, play, rest and creativity had all been pushed aside. His perfectionist tendencies made every task feel like a test, and every rejection a personal indictment, causing him to become depleted as his energy, confidence and joy became eroded.

Yet within the fog, there were clues to what restored him. We explored the concept of embodiment, a developing and radical theory that states that our bodies and physical interactions with the world do much of our thinking for us, rather than us having to rely solely on complex mental processing in the brain. For this to be effective, Ivan had to be able to listen in. Given his constantly stressed state, both mentally and physically, I knew he needed to use some techniques to help him become calmer and more balanced. Ivan was already working with a therapist who had taught him grounding breaths, which I encouraged him to use. I taught him a practice called orienting, which also helped (see Chapter 7 for details on both techniques). Once he was able to become calmer, Ivan began to recognise that he could tune into the messages and insights from his body. All he had to do was decode them and use those energetic insights to help him make wise choices. As a result of listening to himself more consciously, one of the most significant moments came as we worked through the Energy Mapping activity (see full exercise later in this chapter). A deceptively simple exercise, it involved Ivan splitting activities into two lists, those that drained him and those that energised him. We also explored other elements: people, place and time using the same approach. The result was striking. "I realised that writing cover letters, coding under pressure, even networking events – I always leave those feeling flat," he said. "But when I'm exploring ideas, solving a problem creatively, or talking about how people think, I feel alive again." As some coaching questions also helped him to uncover, ultimately, his behaviour all hinged on perceptions of risk. His original thinking was that a job was the safest way to gain a visa and the personal and professional security that he wanted – but it simply was not working and was making him depleted, unhappy and even more at risk.

He went back to a moment we had explored earlier when we began to discuss how, when he was feeling energised, he was in a state of flow in those immersive moments where time seems to disappear and energy flows naturally. "When I'm making art with AI tools, or when I'm tinkering with algorithms to shape images, I lose track of time. That's my zone."

Until then, he had treated those moments as leisure, not something he could develop into a career. But seeing them mapped clearly became his big turning point. It marked the first time he gave himself permission to consider that perhaps his best work might come not from pushing through depletion, but from aligning with the pull of positive energy.

This was the beginning of a more profound shift, not just away from burnout-inducing tasks, but towards work that matched his intrinsic motivation and natural strengths.

We explored the intersection of his technical and creative interests: AI and art; computational creativity, emotionally intelligent systems. It was a different world from consulting or traditional data science, but it clearly lit him up. Soon after, Ivan discovered a relevant PhD opportunity at a London university. It gave him a thread of curiosity to follow, which confirmed that he loved the subject. Despite it having a major corporate sponsorship, which would also give him a significant opportunity, something did not feel right. Together we identified that it was having to be in an academic environment with the risk of the work he was doing becoming obsolete by the time he passed his viva.

We continued to work on helping Ivan to identify patterns in the way he thought and how he viewed the world. It was finally the right moment for him to complete the GET2 (General Enterprising Tendency) assessment developed by Dr Sally Caird of Durham Business School, which measures five entrepreneurial attributes: the need for achievement, autonomy, creative tendency, calculated risk-taking and locus of control. Ivan's results revealed high scores in autonomy, creative tendency and calculated risk-taking, all significant indicators of entrepreneurial potential. These were not things he had named before, but now they made sense. "I think I've been trying to force myself into jobs I think I should want," he said. "But maybe I need to build something myself instead." We did not rush to find answers. Instead, we focused on restoration. Ivan began a daily practice of grounding breathwork and meditation to help manage his emotional state. He created a values-aligned mind map of career options. He joined the start-up scene at the university where he did his master's, started exploring a range of different AI tools, and rebuilt his CV reflecting his entrepreneurial abilities and previous experience. This now reflected the *authentic* Ivan – the person who cared about helping people access their creative potential, not just crunching numbers for the sake of business insights and profit.

One of his most powerful reflections came during our session on purpose. He wrote: "I want to design AI solutions that help people connect to their creativity and think more clearly. I want my work to expand human potential, not just automate tasks." It took several sessions to reach this point – a long way from where we started.

By our last session, Ivan was exploring multiple entrepreneurial ideas, each rooted in his desire to contribute meaningfully without depleting himself. He had also made peace with uncertainty. "I don't have to have it all figured out," he said. "I just need to follow the work that energises me."

A few weeks later, Ivan sent me an update in which he said, "I decided to follow my passion and build my startup around the art and AI space, and it was the best decision… I have been applying to some incubators and just got invited to an interview stage for one of them to pitch my idea!"

Ivan's story is a clear illustration of what depletion looks like in a high-functioning achiever. It does not always present itself in a dramatic way. More often, it appears as quiet fatigue, chronic indecision or the dimming of once-bright passions. The way back is not to push harder, but to pause, listen and reconnect with what matters. Ivan not only managed to recover his energy. He rewrote his story so that he is now driven, not drained, tuned in and feeling focused and fulfilled.

*****

Using the ABCDE model to help Ivan move forward

Activating event
As we know, Ivan experienced repeated professional setbacks after completing his master's degree in the UK. Despite submitting over 40 applications and investing massive effort into tailored CVs, networking and interview preparation, he was repeatedly rejected, ghosted or passed over, all while under pressure from a visa which was running out of time. This cycle left him feeling flat, confused and increasingly depleted.

Beliefs
Ivan held several unhelpful core and conditional beliefs:

- *"If I work hard enough, I should succeed."*

- *"A secure job is the only way to gain long-term safety and a visa."*

- *"Taking time to rest or do things I enjoy is unproductive or indulgent."*

- *"If I don't get a job soon, I'll have failed."*

- *"My worth depends on being efficient and productive."*

- *"Following my curiosity isn't practical."*

These beliefs were driven by perfectionistic behaviour, combined with a desire to minimise the risk of losing his visa status in the UK and drove him to overwork continually.

Consequences

Ivan began to really feel the emotional, cognitive and behavioural consequences of these beliefs. His self-doubt grew as his confidence was eroded through repeated knockbacks, which led to him struggling to make decisions clearly. Each time he invested large amounts of energy and time in applications and interviews, which resulted in near misses or outright rejection or being ghosted by employers, his level of frustration and helplessness increased. The harder he worked, the more his perfectionism drove him to be hyper-analytical, necessitating even more effort. These cycles of intense effort caused him to experience repeated periods of depletion where he felt emotionally exhausted and physically tired, separating him from his true self and what gave him joy and meaning. The end point was feelings of stagnation compared with peers and an increasing sense of isolation.

Dispute

Through coaching, Ivan began to challenge and reframe his existing beliefs. We started by exploring whether his current path (high-effort job-seeking) was the only route to visa security and fulfilment. That enabled us to discuss whether success had to come from conforming to the system, or whether it could come from alignment with his unique strengths and energy. Identifying what he truly valued using the Values Wheel helped us to explore how his fear of risk was leading to greater long-term risk and enabled him to recognise what he was experiencing: depletion, unhappiness and professional drift. Exploring themes around meaning and purpose, which came from his values, enabled him to recognise that purpose, energy and progress emerge from alignment with who he is, not exhaustion from trying to fit the system. Similarly, completing the GET2 test helped Ivan to see his entrepreneurial qualities.

The breakthrough came through energy mapping: identifying what drained him in terms of people (closed minds), place (slow pace and progress), time (e.g. coding for others under pressure) and tasks (e.g. writing cover letters) versus what energised him (e.g. like-minded people, solving problems creatively, art and AI). This gave Ivan permission to reconnect with his strengths and what made him feel most alive, effective and joyful by finding his flow states.

Effect

With insight and reflection, Ivan replaced his unhelpful beliefs with more supportive ones, including:

- *"What energises me is a better compass than what impresses others."*

- *"Success is sustainable when it comes from alignment, not depletion."*

- *"My work can be meaningful, creative, and practical."*

- *"Rest and reconnection aren't weaknesses – they are strategic."*

- *"Entrepreneurship isn't riskier – it may be the more authentic, energising path."*

- *"I don't need to have everything figured out. I just need to follow what lights me up."*

These new beliefs opened the door to purpose-led entrepreneurship and helped Ivan reframe his identity from failing jobseeker to creative technologist and change-maker. He is now pitching for the partners and finance he needs to get his AI start-up off the ground.

Activities to create changes in depletion thinking and behaviour

The following activities are designed to help clients work with rather than against who they are naturally in terms of energy, physiology, psychology and body clocks. The activities do not include strengths-based content, as this is a well-established and familiar concept across career development and HR practice. Instead, the activities focus on less common, more emergent areas of practice.

ACTIVITY 1: ENERGY MAPPING: CHARTING WHAT FUELS AND DEPLETES YOU

As we saw in Ivan's story, our energy gets enriched or depleted in different ways. Helping clients who are experiencing depletion to understand their own unique energy patterns provides the first step in helping them to break the cycle. This Energy Mapping activity uses the core principles of all five theories by helping clients to: recognise energy drains before they become chronic, rebalance their environment and choices to support recovery and reallocate attention to areas that naturally energise and sustain them across four key dimensions. Raising awareness of their needs means that clients can make more effective choices and decisions that protect their energy and support their wellbeing. Explaining this to your client provides the why and benefits of this activity.

Step 1: What makes a great day

Invite your client to think back to a day at work or study that they really enjoyed.

Encourage them to describe the day in detail. They may also find it helpful to review it using their preferred sensory mode:

- **Visual thinkers** may find it helpful to re-run the "movie" of the day in their mind's eye.
- **Auditory thinkers** may want to replay conversations, sounds or tones.
- **Kinaesthetic thinkers** may opt to concentrate on how the day felt, physically or emotionally.

As they reflect, it is helpful to prompt them to consider:

- Who they were with.
- What tasks they were doing.
- Where they were.
- When in the day they felt most alive or effective.

This exploration helps them tune into what naturally energises or sustains them, so they are ready for the next step.

Step 2: Four-dimensional energy mapping

Ask your client to draw the following table using the same four categories of: People, Place, Tasks and Time.

	Energisers	Energy thieves
People		
Place		
Tasks		
Time		

Now ask them to list what fuels or steals their energy in each category. Encourage them to use colour-coding or emojis if this would work best for them. Here are some helpful coaching questions for each of the dimensions:

For People:

- Energisers: *"Who uplifts or inspires you?"*
- Drains: *"Who leaves you feeling tense or depleted?"*

For Place:

- Energisers: *"Which environments help you feel calm, focused or creative?"*
- Drains: *"Which spaces feel noisy, chaotic or uninspiring?"*

For Tasks:

- Energisers: *"What activities give you flow or meaning?"*
- Drains: *"What feels monotonous, pointless or overly stressful?"*

For Time:

- Energisers: *"When do you feel most alert and effective?"*
- Drains: *"When do you tend to feel foggy, scattered or fatigued?"*

Step 3: Integrating reflections

Here are some prompts to help your client reflect on how they use their energy:

- *"Which category has the biggest effect on your energy?"*
- *"What overlaps can you see between your "great day" and your energisers?"*

You can also adapt this activity to suit different learning styles. Depending on the setting and time available, the client might choose to storyboard, sketch, role-play, journal, write a poem or even compose a short song to capture what energises and depletes them most.

ACTIVITY 2: TIME TO THRIVE: USING YOUR NATURAL RHYTHMS

As we have all discovered, our brains and bodies are simply not built for nonstop performance at lightning speeds. This activity encourages clients to become familiar with their own natural biological and cognitive rhythms and cycles (circadian, chronotype and ultradian) and put them to work every day so they can get the most out of life without becoming depleted.

Here is a helpful way to introduce this three-part activity.

Step 1: Understanding your body clock

We are all governed by **circadian rhythms**, the universal internal timing system that influences the 24-hour cycle of physiological functions (sleep, wake, hormone release, etc.). This is often what people mean when they talk about body clocks.

Understanding your body clock will help you understand and align with your natural circadian rhythm so you can optimise energy, mood, focus and recovery while at the same time protecting yourself from depletion. It takes time to understand your natural daily energy rhythm.

The best way to do this is to rate your energy, mood and focus at regular intervals across the next five or so days using the table below.

As you can see, you simply need to score how you feel about each of these themes out of 10, where 1 is low and 10 is high. Then remember to note anything of relevance, for example, relating to meals and what you ate, hydration, movement, tasks, interruptions and so on.

Time slot	Energy (1–10)	Mood (1–10)	Focus (1–10)	Notes (e.g. meals, movement, tasks, interruptions)
6.00-9.00 a.m.				
9.00-12.00 p.m.				
12.00-3.00 p.m.				
3.00-6.00 p.m.				
6.00-9.00 p.m.				
9.00 p.m.-bedtime				

As a practitioner, when you are working with your client and depending on time, you may want to work through the previous day together and then assign days 2–5 as a post-coaching activity for a deeper dive in your next session.

If you want to use this activity in a group setting in particular, it may also be easier to use sad, neutral and happy emojis on Post-it notes on flip chart sheets or digital whiteboards in the room or online using anonymous survey tools like Mentimeter or Padlet.

As the client is working, you may want to use some prompt questions to get them thinking, to build task confidence and awareness quickly such as these,:

- *"How energised did you feel first thing?"*
- *"What kind of tasks were easiest mid-morning?"*
- *"Was there a noticeable dip at any point?"*

Once they have tracked their energy, mood and focus, ideally over several days, encourage your client to step back and notice the patterns, particularly in relation to when they tend to function at their best and worst. The following questions, which work equally well as coaching questions or as journalling prompts, are useful for this:

- *"How did the previous day's events affect your energy first thing today?"*
- *"What kind of tasks were easiest mid-morning?"*
- *"Was there a noticeable dip at any point?"*

Step 2: Identifying your personal energy patterns

This part of the activity is designed to encourage clients to build on what they discovered about their body clocks by looking at the first of two finer sets of rhythms, **chronotypes**. These indicate our genetically influenced natural inclination to be one of three types:

- A **morning person or lark**. Larks are early to bed and early to rise, and feel most focused in the morning, preferring to get big tasks done early. They may feel more sluggish in the afternoons.
- An **evening person or night owl**. Owls come alive in the evening and feel sluggish in the mornings. Their peak focus and creativity often occur late in the afternoon or even at night.
- An **intermediate type or what we could call a hummingbird**. Like the bird, these are people who are active throughout the day, often from just after dawn until dusk. Unlike larks or owls, they don't strongly favour early mornings or late evenings but maintain steady energy during daylight hours, which feels relatively balanced. They are alert mid-morning, constant through the afternoon and able to wind down in the evening.

Most people are a balance rather than an extreme in their chronotype.

When there is misalignment between our chronotype and our work time, it reduces performance and increases burnout. An example of a mismatch is night owls who have to work early. When there is flexible scheduling that respects chronotypes, engagement, accuracy and health are all boosted.

Here are some questions to use to help your client uncover their chronotype:

- *"What time do you naturally wake up and feel alert on a day with no obligations?"*
- *"When do you feel most productive or 'in flow'?"*
- *"If you had to do focused work, when would you choose to do it?"*
- *"When do you feel like your energy dips or crashes?"*
- *"What time do you naturally want to go to sleep?"*

These questions can also be turned into journalling prompts to keep a client on track after the session.

ACTIVITY 3: CREATING YOUR IDEAL DAILY RHYTHM

According to researchers, if we go too long without breaks, our executive functioning begins to decline as prolonged mental effort leads to cognitive and decision fatigue. This impairs our ability to make sound judgements, control impulses and reduces our motivation. Alternating demanding tasks with breaks reduces errors and preserves cognitive control. This is where the second of the finer types of rhythms we have, called **ultradian rhythms,** play their part. Research shows that our brains follow 90–120-minute cycles of alertness and rest. Respecting these ultradian rhythms by alternating periods of focus with short recovery breaks enhances cognitive function, metabolic health and sustained performance throughout the day, even without taking circadian cues into account.

If we understand and apply these personal rhythms to our natural energy, we can use that understanding to work more effectively. When we work with deep focus and without distraction during our natural energy peaks, we can work smarter, not just harder. The benefits are many: increased productivity, greater creativity, reduced mental fatigue and better decision-making.

The following activity enables clients to create a template for their working day, which aligns with both their energy and their natural rhythms:

Step 1: Map your natural focus-recovery cycle

Invite your client to reflect on their day-to-day experience of concentration, fatigue and motivation. They may not have language for "ultradian rhythms" yet, but most will recognise the feeling of mental fog or impulsive email-checking after long stints of focus. At this point, it is helpful to introduce the concept of ultradian rhythms. The following coaching questions offer ways to guide and support both self-observation and discussion so they can recognise their own cognition rhythms:

- *"How long can you typically focus before your attention starts to dip?"*
- *"What are the first signs that you need a break?"*
- *(e.g. re-reading things, zoning out, snack cravings, irritability, head tension)*
- *"What type of break helps you reset best?"*
- *(e.g. movement, hydration, music, sunlight, breathing, conversation)*
- *"What steps can you take to protect time and energy for activities which have both high value and high meaning?"*

Once a client has estimated or identified their ideal cycle length, they are ready to move on to the next step.

Step 2: Creating your ideal day template

Help your client to create an outline timetable which either starts from the time they wake up and ends when they go to bed, or one which just focuses on the working day, depending on what they prefer to do. Then, ask them to identify blocks of time which reflect their preferred cycle length for focus tasks, and breaks for energy recovery and building energy, using what they identified in step one. Encourage them to add a "Planned Break Activity." For some clients, this may mean getting up and stretching or going for a walk. For others, it may be playing a piece of music or a short meditation that they need to reset their emotions or reading something unrelated to their current activities. For most, it is likely to include some form of hydration and healthy nutrition. Finally, encourage your client to develop their listening inside skills so they can capture valuable insights in the "Notes/reflections" column.

Here is an example based on an Ideal Working Day template to help.

Time	Focus task block	Energy state (self-assessed)	Planned break activity	Notes/ reflections
8.00-9.30 a.m.				
9.30-9.50 a.m.	Break	-		
9.50-11.20 a.m.				
11.20-11.40 a.m.	Break	-		
11.40-1.00 p.m.				
1.00-2.00 p.m.	Lunch + Rest	-		
2.00-3.30 p.m.				
3.30-3.50 p.m.	Break	-		
3.50-5.00 p.m.				

Your client may also need to consider any different workday lengths, parenting/caring commitments or hybrid schedules, which will affect their timetable.

Encouraging them to use the template to plan out activities to test the plan in the following week and stick to it as much as possible will pay dividends.

> ## Step 3: Embedding practice through reflection
>
> According to researchers at UCL, it takes 66 days to form a new habit. So once clients have tried working this way for a while, they may need some further encouragement to embed their new approach. Here are some reflective prompts they can use during the trial period and beyond:
>
> - *"What happened when you respected your natural rhythm?"*
> - *"Which types of breaks helped most – and which didn't?"*
> - *"How did your motivation, decision-making or emotional state change?"*
> - *"What barriers got in the way – and what might you change tomorrow?"*
>
> You could also encourage them to complete a weekly review using this or similar journalling prompts:
>
> *"How well did I respect my focus and recovery rhythms this week – and what impact has this had on my energy, clarity, or resilience?"*
>
> If you are working with neurodivergent clients or those in high-stakes work cultures, you may need to co-create microbreak strategies or help the client to advocate for protected focus blocks.
>
> This activity works well in 1:1 and group coaching, either on its own or with one or both previous depletion prevention activities.

Summary

As you have seen, while temporary energy fluctuations are natural, depletion becomes a thief when sustained effort consistently drains our mental, emotional and physical resources faster than they can be replenished, creating a progressive spiral of diminished capacity and motivation. When clients become trapped in patterns of surface acting, misaligned effort and resource overinvestment without adequate return, they sacrifice authenticity, clarity and sustainable wellbeing. As neuroscience reveals, chronic depletion fundamentally alters brain chemistry and neural regulation, weakening prefrontal control while heightening emotional reactivity and reducing motivation. Meanwhile, the psychological theories demonstrate how cumulative resource loss, failed self-regulation cycles and emotional labour create compounding exhaustion that extends far beyond simple tiredness. Left unchecked, depletion erodes decision-making capacity, wears away identity and undermines an individual's ability to pursue meaningful work aligned with their authentic and natural strengths, values and energies. Without strategic coaching interventions, those who persist in depleting patterns will find themselves falling victim to the sixth of our Seven Career Thieves: the Thief of Disconnection, which we will explore together in the next chapter.

5. The Thief of Depletion
At a glance

Working definition: "A gradual loss of mental, emotional, or physical energy due to stress, effort or self-control. This makes it harder to concentrate, make decisions, maintain motivation, or perform effectively at work or in learning environments."

Key theories and models:

1. **Ego Depletion Theory (Baumeister et al., 1998):** Self-control draws on limited mental resources that get depleted with use, reducing willpower, focus and persistence until recovery through rest.
2. **Conservation of Resources Theory (Hobfoll, 1989):** Stress and burnout result from loss or threatened loss of personal, social or material resources that individuals strive to protect and restore.

Impact and context:

Lowers performance, weakens self-control, reduces stress resilience, leads to burnout and health risks.

Women report higher emotional exhaustion, especially in people-focused professions.

Neurodivergent individuals experience intensified depletion due to masking and environmental mismatch.

High in finance, law, consulting (mental); public sector/education (resource scarcity); entrepreneurs (isolation/uncertainty).

- **Early career:** Inexperience and pressure.
- **Mid-career:** Greater stability but stagnation risk.
- **Late career:** Physical decline.

Warning signs:

- **Mental slowness:** "I just feel... slow. Like I'm not progressing."
- **Decision fatigue:** Simple choices become complex and overwhelming.
- **Motivation loss:** Tasks that once energised now feel effortful.
- **Emotional numbness:** Reduced capacity to feel joy or satisfaction.
- **Chronic fatigue:** Persistent tiredness despite adequate rest.
- **Reduced resilience:** Small setbacks feel disproportionately difficult.
- **Identity confusion:** "I don't recognise myself anymore."

When the energy tanks are empty

3. **Action Regulation Theory (Hacker and Frese, 2017):** People plan and execute goal-directed behaviour through cognitive regulation. Poor work design increases mental strain and depletion.
4. **Allostatic Load Theory (McEwen and Stellar, 1993, McEwen, 1998):** Chronic stress accumulates biological "wear and tear," weakening regulation systems and increasing depletion risk without recovery.
5. **Emotional Labour Theory (Hochschild, 1983 and Grandey, 2000):** Managing emotions to meet job demands. Surface acting (faking emotions) leads to emotional dissonance and authenticity loss.

Neuroscience:

Depletion fundamentally alters brain chemistry and neural regulation, affecting how we think, feel and act:

- **Prefrontal cortex:** Weakened top-down control reduces self-regulation and impulse management.
- **Amygdala:** Becomes hyperreactive to negative stimuli with reduced PFC connectivity.
- **Anterior insula:** Monitors perceived effort cost, shifting the brain towards rest or avoidance.
- **Neurochemical changes:** Glutamate accumulates, dopamine/serotonin drop, stress hormones rise.

Brain doesn't simply "run out" of resources – it shifts into a protective state, recalibrating motivation systems towards rest and recovery.

Key coaching activities:

1. **Energy Mapping:** Charts what fuels and depletes across four dimensions: People, Place, Tasks and Time for conscious energy management.
2. **Natural Rhythms Alignment:** How to use circadian, chronotype and ultradian cycles to optimise performance while preventing depletion.
3. **Embodied Awareness Practice:** Tune into body wisdom and somatic markers to make energy-aligned choices and decisions.

Core takeaway: Shift from **energy drain** to **sustainable alignment**.

6 | The Thief of Disconnection

When connection and purpose are lost

> "Every human has a true, genuine, authentic self.
> The trauma is the disconnection from it.
> The healing is the reconnection with it."
>
> Gabor Maté, Hungarian-born Canadian physician, author and speaker.

Brian's story

Brian was in his early 50s when things started to unravel. His worried wife encouraged him to get some career coaching to help him navigate his way through what was clearly a challenging period for him.

A seasoned leader in the pharmaceuticals industry specialising in project management, he had taken on a senior role with a £150K per annum salary in a start-up led by a former CEO he knew. At first, he brought his usual strengths: clarity, structure and accountability. He worked his magic and turned chaos into order.

But as the business shifted, so did his role.

He was kept on the payroll for three months with a loose Merger and Acquisition remit, paid well but largely unused. "I'm being paid a fortune to do nothing," he said. "I've started reading my Kindle for four hours a day."

His days were quiet. The job was US-facing, so he worked alone, from home, at odd hours. There were few meetings and even fewer decisions for him to get involved with. Due to the time zone difference, he had been forced to step back from coaching the local youth football team.

It was clear that while his confidence had not crashed totally, it was slowly but surely being eroded, particularly as a high achiever who thrived on recognition.

"I feel like I'm disappearing," he admitted. "I don't know what I'm doing anymore."

A formal redundancy notice was issued. His boss hinted at a part-time contract, but the follow-up never came. "He just confirmed my redundancy by text," Brian said. "And then they deleted my email account."

He described the loss not just in terms of role, but of rhythm and relationships. "It's the lack of stimulation. The lack of people." Familiar networks had dissolved overnight. "I don't miss the business, but I do miss the sense of being part of something."

His energy was low; he was sleeping poorly, and his motivation to look for work had vanished. "I'm either all in, or I shut down," he said. He was beginning to show signs of burnout and seemed depressed, not from overwork, but from isolation and misalignment.

When we first spoke, he was wrestling with conflicting desires: the pull of early retirement versus the need to stay useful; the comfort of security versus the ache for something more meaningful. "The more I think about it," he said, "the more I want to change."

We talked about some other options, mainly related to various forms of self-employment, as the corporate environment jaded him. He experimented with different ideas, including helping friends with their fencing business and taking on a zero-hour sports facilitator role to see if he wanted to become a personal trainer, but nothing felt right. As Brian's confidence shrank, so did his career horizons.

He wanted autonomy, respect, challenge and to work in ways that made a difference. "I don't want to report to people who know less than me." As a self-confessed high achiever, he was not being arrogant; he just wanted to work with other like-minded professionals in an environment where ability, integrity and trust mattered.

"I want to do something that matters. Something where I'm busy, with people I like... and have time to think. Not glued to a screen all day."

Rather than pushing for quick answers, we began by helping Brian restore a sense of regular rhythm and wellbeing. I encouraged him to start going back to the gym five mornings a week again, partly for his health, but mainly to help him feel less isolated. He also decided to pick up coaching the youth football team again. "It's just good to see people again," he said. "And coaching too... I'd forgotten how good that feels."

The change was important. He was getting out of his head and back into the community. "I'd lost that," he said. "That feeling of being part of something bigger."

It was at this point that Brian's coaching journey began in earnest.

*****

So, what is disconnection?

Disconnection can be described as a psychological state in which individuals experience a profound sense of detachment from meaning, recognition and their authentic selves. This state often leads to emotional withdrawal and reduced engagement with work and life. Although there is no single, universally agreed definition, research from the National Institute of Mental Health on social disconnection, along with workplace psychology literature, highlights three progressive stages in how disconnection typically unfolds.

1. **Loss of meaning and purpose** occurs when individuals begin to feel that their work or life lacks deeper significance. Motivation and direction begin to fade, making it harder to sustain energy, commitment or hope for the future.
2. **Emotional or social withdrawal** often follows, presenting as retreating from relationships or suppressing emotional expression. This is frequently a self-protective response in environments where individuals feel undervalued, misunderstood or alienated.
3. **Erosion of identity and engagement** develops as meaningful roles, routines or recognition fall away. Over time, people begin to lose touch with who they are and what they stand for, leading to a slow but steady disengagement from both work and self.

When it comes to **personality**, insights from the OCEAN Big Five model show that certain traits increase vulnerability to disconnection, while others offer protection:

High Neuroticism increases risk across all three stages of disconnection. Individuals high in this trait are more prone to interpreting neutral events as threatening, and often experience heightened emotional reactivity, anxiety and rumination, leading to poor engagement, especially under uncertainty or stress.

Low Openness contributes to loss of meaning and identity erosion by limiting cognitive flexibility, curiosity and the ability to reframe or find new sources of purpose.

Low Conscientiousness undermines sustained engagement by reducing self-regulation, persistence and goal-directed behaviour, making it harder to maintain a sense of progress or structure when routines fall away.

Low Agreeableness and Extraversion increase risk during the withdrawal stage, as individuals with these traits may be more socially avoidant or reactive, making them more likely to retreat from relationships, team dynamics or help-seeking.

By contrast, the most resilient personality profile combines **low Neuroticism** with **high Conscientiousness and Openness**, offering emotional stability, focus and adaptability.

Importantly, research consistently shows that **Conscientiousness** is the strongest overall predictor of job performance, while **Openness** is the most significant predictor of employee engagement across diverse roles and environments.

This suggests interventions should be tailored to personality profiles, with high-neuroticism individuals needing additional emotional support and low-openness individuals requiring structured approaches to finding new meaning and purpose.

Why should we be worried about disconnection?

Disconnection, whether from people, purpose or one's own sense of self, has a dual impact. While in some instances it can cause real harm, disconnection can also act as a motivator for change.

As we saw in Brian's case, it is primarily harmful, undermining wellbeing, performance, relationships and self-worth. Left unaddressed, it becomes a serious threat to wellbeing, performance and retention, especially among high achievers. Disconnection erodes the clear psychological safety, and wellbeing, evident in safe, connected environments which is essential for organisational health, innovation and personal fulfilment.

When acknowledged and addressed, however, disconnection challenges can also motivate meaningful reflection and positive change, prompting individuals and organisations to restore what matters most: connection, purpose and recognition.

In the **workplace**, disconnection is evident when people disengage from their work, colleagues and the organisational mission. It appears as withdrawal, lack of initiative, poor communication, low morale and ultimately, increased turnover and burnout. Disconnection is a leading predictor of disengagement, presenteeism and quiet quitting. According to professors Anthony C. Klots and Mark C. Bolino in the Harvard Business Review, this is a phenomenon where *"quiet quitters continue to fulfill their primary responsibilities, but they're less willing to engage in activities known as citizenship behaviors: no more staying late, showing up early, or attending non-mandatory meetings."*

The latest figures in Gallup's State of the Global Workplace 2025 report and data confirm the global cost of lost productivity due to falling employee engagement in 2024 as being US$438 billion. Worldwide, only 21% of employees globally are actively engaged at work, while the majority report feeling emotionally detached or indifferent to their jobs. Although the European employee engagement figure is currently slightly higher at 23%, in the UK only 1 in 10 people are fully engaged intellectually and emotionally. Disconnection significantly raises the risk of burnout and attrition, particularly when workers no longer see how their contribution matters or feel excluded from meaningful decision-making. From an organisational perspective, when individuals feel micromanaged, underused or isolated, they begin to question their value, which can erode confidence and spark a slow drift into self-doubt and withdrawal. Teams also suffer as a consequence.

The absence of meaningful connection not only impacts employees' mood and motivation but also increases stress-related cortisol levels, accelerating emotional fatigue. The stakes are particularly high for high achievers. Many define themselves through contribution and recognition, so when work no longer aligns with their values or fails to offer a sense of impact, it can trigger an identity crisis. What might look like quiet withdrawal on the surface may, in reality, signal deep psychological misalignment and existential crisis underneath.

In **education**, disconnection leads to academic disengagement, emotional withdrawal, lower achievement, increased risk of failure, and teacher disengagement. Disconnected students may appear apathetic, withdrawn or display behavioural issues. Educators who feel unsupported may experience burnout and impaired relationships. Systemic and environmental factors like school climate and culture, remote and hybrid learning and the power of connection can also contribute to disconnection.

The relationship between **age** and disconnection is both complex and context-dependent. In adolescence and early adulthood, disconnection is often driven by loneliness, a lack of purpose and digital overexposure, with social comparison and fear of missing out (FOMO) contributing to emotional detachment. In midlife, juggling multiple roles, such as parenting, caregiving for ageing parents and managing careers and relationships, makes finding space for connection and self-reflection more difficult. This period is also associated with the well-documented "midlife dip" in life satisfaction. In later life, disconnection may result from loss of role (e.g. retirement), bereavement, physical health challenges, additional caregiving responsibilities or shrinking social networks. Older adults are particularly vulnerable to chronic loneliness, which is linked to increased risks of cognitive decline, depression and early mortality.

When it comes to **gender,** disconnection manifests differently for men and women at work, and is shaped by societal expectations. Often encouraged to prioritise relationships and emotional openness, women may feel disconnection most acutely as exclusion, relational loss or emotional isolation, especially in environments where their contributions are undervalued. In contrast, men, typically raised to emphasise independence and stoicism, may respond to disconnection by withdrawing emotionally or being reluctant to seek support, even when it is needed. Workplace culture can reinforce these patterns. Women in male-centric roles may experience marginalisation, while men in caring professions may suppress emotion to fit in. Both groups face challenges here, with women sometimes dismissed as "too sensitive" and men fearing stigma for showing vulnerability.

Neurodivergent individuals, including those with autism, ADHD, dyslexia and other neurological differences, often experience workplace disconnection due to environments designed for neurotypical communication and processing styles. Sensory overload, communication mismatches and pressure to mask authentic behaviours can lead to exclusion and marginalisation. This disconnection can present as increased loneliness, mental health challenges and barriers to recognition despite often bringing many valuable strengths including attention to detail, innovative thinking and specialised expertise. Inclusive cultures that recognise neurodivergence as difference rather than deficit, can significantly reduce disconnection through sensory accommodations, flexible communication styles and clear expectations.

Socio-economic status (SES) and disconnection are also closely linked. Individuals from lower SES backgrounds often face greater exposure to social exclusion, stigma, financial instability and limited access to supportive opportunities, all of which increase vulnerability to disconnection. This disconnection may show up as reduced participation in community or cultural life, feelings of powerlessness or disengagement from work and relationships. It is also associated with higher rates of depression, anxiety and chronic stress. In contrast, individuals from higher SES groups tend to benefit from greater autonomy, broader social networks and access to mental health and career support, factors that help buffer against disconnection and support a stronger sense of belonging.

From a **cultural and ethnic perspective,** disconnection is again a complex issue with minority and marginalised groups often facing significantly heightened risk due to social exclusion, discrimination and underrepresentation. Cultural norms shape how disconnection is both experienced and expressed. Collectivist cultures that value close-knit community ties may frame disconnection as shame or collective disappointment, while individualist cultures that emphasise autonomy may interpret it as personal failure or inadequacy. Language barriers, microaggressions and what can be the exhausting work of cultural code-switching can intensify feelings of isolation, particularly in predominantly majority-culture environments. As a result, disconnection may manifest as withdrawal, self-censorship, disengagement or masking of authentic cultural identity. Systemic and historical factors such as colonisation, racial discrimination and the complex interplay of intersecting identities can further amplify these experiences across generations. Protective factors include strong cultural identity, supportive community networks and cultural traditions that reinforce belonging and collective resilience. Organisational practices like affinity groups, mentorship programmes, inclusive policies and culturally responsive support can promote visibility and authentic connection.

Wherever disconnection appears, recognising and addressing it early, through coaching, meaningful dialogue and values-aligned planning, can prevent long-term damage. Re-establishing the underlying missing elements of meaning and purpose, recognition and self-connection provides the pathway back from disconnection in both professional and personal contexts, restoring clarity, belonging and purpose-led direction.

Disconnection and sectors

A significant challenge across all industries, disconnection manifests differently depending on sector-specific dynamics, work structures and cultural norms. While some sectors naturally foster connection through collaborative practices, others create environments where isolation and disengagement are more likely to develop. Understanding these sector-specific patterns helps organisations to proactively address disconnection risks and individuals to make wise choices that work for them:

- **Remote-heavy and tech sectors** like **IT**, **consulting** and **digital services** face heightened disconnection risks due to limited face-to-face interaction, digital overload and reduced spontaneous connection opportunities, leading to social isolation, reduced team cohesion and difficulty building authentic workplace relationships.
- **Highly competitive sectors** such as **finance**, **law** and **sales** often prioritise individual achievement and performance metrics, creating cultures of rivalry and limited psychological safety that can drive emotional withdrawal, surface-level interactions and fear-based working relationships.
- **Shift-based and gig economy sectors**, including **healthcare**, **manufacturing**, **hospitality** and **retail**, create structural barriers to stable relationship-building through irregular schedules, high turnover and fragmented teams, leading to feelings of invisibility, transactional interactions and lack of workplace belonging.
- **People-centred professions** like **education**, **social work** and **well-resourced healthcare** can provide natural buffers against disconnection through shared purpose, teamwork and interpersonal focus, though chronic stress and under-resourcing can quickly erode these protective factors.
- **Creative and mission-driven sectors** such as **nonprofits**, **start-ups** and **research** organisations often foster strong connections through shared values and a collaborative spirit, but may risk cliquishness, overwork or burnout if boundaries and inclusion are not actively managed.
- **Rapidly changing sectors** undergoing digital transformation or frequent restructuring, including **media**, **communications** and **retail**, may inadvertently increase disconnection through job insecurity, loss of familiar routines and constant adaptation demands that disrupt established relationships and team dynamics.

Disconnection becomes problematic when sector characteristics consistently undermine the basic human needs for autonomy, competence and relatedness, the core components highlighted by Self-Determination Theory. When entrenched in organisational cultures, disconnection reduces innovation, increases turnover and compromises both individual wellbeing and collective performance across all industry contexts.

Entrepreneurship can present a heightened risk of disconnection, particularly during early and high-pressure phases of business development. Founders often work alone or in small teams, especially at the beginning, which limits informal interaction and increases the likelihood of social and emotional isolation. This is particularly true for solo entrepreneurs and those whose business model centres on remote or solitary work. Unlike traditional employment, external feedback can be delayed, ambiguous or absent. Without clear signals of progress or recognition, founders may begin to question their own judgement or value, leading to a gradual disconnection from others, their purpose or even themselves. The highs and lows of business cycles, coupled with long hours, emotional investment and financial uncertainty, can lead to self-doubt, impaired decision-making and burnout. Psychologically, entrepreneurs are often high in achievement motivation, autonomy and risk tolerance, traits that support innovation, but also create vulnerability. When the boundary between personal identity and business identity blurs, failures or setbacks can feel deeply personal. As a result, some entrepreneurs experience identity disruption, emotional withdrawal or an over-reliance on performance to justify self-worth. Despite these risks, many entrepreneurs find deep purpose and meaning in their ventures, sometimes reporting a stronger sense of connection to their work than traditional employees. Common strategies to prevent disconnection include maintaining work-life boundaries, cultivating support networks and engaging with like-minded peers. Founder communities, accelerators and co-working spaces can provide both practical help and a renewed sense of belonging.

Disconnection across the career lifespan

As disconnection develops, it affects different stages of the career lifespan in distinctive ways, often reflecting shifts in roles, identity and sources of meaning over time.

Early careers: Here, disconnection often arises from a lack of purpose, unclear direction or misalignment between values and roles. Many young professionals take roles that underuse their strengths or misalign with their aspirations, often out of financial necessity, where short-term income outweighs longer-term meaning often creating the commonplace quarter-life crisis. Isolation, especially in entry-level or remote roles, can hinder confidence and community building, while a lack of mentorship leaves many without guidance to navigate towards purposeful careers. Instability in internships, short-term contracts or gig roles can further erode confidence, fuelling self-doubt, imposter syndrome and a deepening sense of drift.

Mid-careers: At this stage, disconnection also often arises from values misalignment or a sense that work no longer reflects who a person is or wants to become. Individuals may continue to perform well outwardly, even as they feel increasingly disconnected, particularly when goals evolve or organisational shifts create misalignment. This stage is often marked by the strain of competing life demands, including caregiving for children, older relatives or others, and career pressures, with little space for renewal. This mid-career dip/crisis phase brings risks of plateau, stalled growth and burnout, especially in environments that undervalue contribution or fail to adapt to an individual's changing needs.

Late careers and retirement: By this third stage, as in Brian's story, disconnection is often driven by a loss of role, status or perceived relevance. Redundancy, age bias or reduced growth opportunities can leave individuals feeling sidelined, especially when transitions are unplanned. Erosion of professional identity, shrinking networks and caregiving demands for spouses or ageing parents may further affect confidence and belonging. Technology gaps and health changes can intensify feelings of exclusion or obsolescence. Yet, this life stage can also bring renewed purpose, particularly when people are supported to mentor, consult or contribute through flexible roles that reflect evolving priorities. Whether disconnection deepens or connection is restored depends on how well individuals can align legacy, autonomy and meaningful contribution, while balancing financial realities and health needs.

Disconnection often signals fundamental misalignment, whether with a specific role or sector, values, belonging or meaning. For achievers, this disconnection can be particularly disorientating when it occurs despite strong performance, creating a paradox where external success masks internal emptiness and questioning of deeply held professional identity. When left unaddressed, this can lead to emotional withdrawal, stalled progression or reactive job changes driven by frustration rather than clarity. Clients may feel stuck, cynical or question their professional identity altogether, as happened with Brian. In these cases, disconnection narrows possibilities and undermines confidence in the future.

The neuroscience of disconnection

Biologically, as a species, we are wired for connection, and it is fundamental to brain health. When individuals experience prolonged disconnection, whether from others, from purpose or even from themselves, measurable changes occur in both brain function and neural wiring.

Key regions in the brain's social network, such as the **medial prefrontal cortex** and **posterior cingulate cortex**, play vital roles in empathy, self-reflection and social understanding. During periods of loneliness or isolation, activity in these areas can diminish, making it harder to read social cues or feel emotionally present in relationships. As these circuits downregulate, people may find it more difficult to relate to others, or even to themselves, deepening the experience of being misunderstood, excluded or adrift.

Disconnection also activates the brain's threat detection systems. When individuals feel left out, judged or rejected, the **amygdala**, the brain's emotional alarm centre, becomes more reactive. This increases vigilance and defensiveness, keeping people on high alert for further social threats and making genuine reconnection feel risky or unsafe.

Brain chemistry

Disconnection is not just a state of mind; it reflects a chemical shift in the brain:

Oxytocin, the "bonding hormone," typically rises during trust-building and close social interaction. When disconnection takes hold, oxytocin levels drop, making it harder to feel safe, close or emotionally available, even in new or supportive environments.

Dopamine, the brain's reward and motivation chemical, also declines. This can reduce the sense of satisfaction in work or social experiences, draining energy and making previously enjoyable activities feel effortful or empty.

Cortisol and **adrenaline**, the body's main stress hormones, increase with prolonged exclusion or social uncertainty. This activates the "fight or flight" response, impairing relaxation, openness and emotional regulation. Over time, this can lead to chronic anxiety, social withdrawal and emotional exhaustion.

BDNF (Brain-Derived Neurotrophic Factor), a key protein for neuroplasticity and emotional resilience, may also decline under long-term social stress. This can affect the brain's ability to adapt, recover or rebuild meaningful relationships after setbacks.

Neurodivergent individuals may experience disconnection differently depending on how their brains process social information and environmental stimuli. Autistic individuals often have different patterns of social brain activity, which can make typical social interactions more tiring in non-accommodating environments. Those with ADHD, autism or AuDHD, may face challenges with sustained attention in social contexts. The stress of masking or adapting to neurotypical expectations can intensify a sense of disconnection. However, these differences are not inherently problematic, as supportive, accommodating environments that recognise diverse neurological styles can promote connection and wellbeing. For example, creating quiet workspaces, offering flexible communication styles or supporting asynchronous collaboration can help reduce disconnection for neurodivergent team members. The key is matching support approaches to individual neurological profiles rather than assuming universal social connection pathways.

Disconnection theory in action

Brian's story of disconnection can be understood through several theoretical lenses. Rather than examining each theory in isolation, we can use his own words and experiences as anchor points to help us explore how different theories collectively illuminate what was happening.

"I feel like I'm disappearing"

This statement captures the collapse of identity and belonging that Brian felt when his role was sidelined.

- **Viktor Frankl's Logotherapy** highlights how the loss of meaning leads to what Frankl called the "existential vacuum," marked by emptiness and disengagement.
- **Axel Honneth's Recognition Theory** frames this as misrecognition: Brian's contributions were devalued, his expertise ignored and his dignity eroded through an impersonal redundancy process.
- **Henri Tajfel and John Turner's Social Identity Theory** explains the identity threat Brian felt of being excluded from his leadership group and stripped of insider status.
- **John Bowlby et al.'s Attachment Theory** highlights that the workplace no longer provided a secure base. Deprived of safety and recognition, Brian's protective response was withdrawal.
- **Urie Bronfenbrenner's Ecological Systems Theory** shows how this disconnection rippled outward, as work alienation strained Brian's relationships at home (microsystem) and was compounded by cultural norms discouraging openness about struggle (macrosystem).

Taken together, Brian's sense of "disappearing" was not just a personal reaction but the intersection of existential, relational, social and systemic forces.

"I'm either all in, or I shut down"

This phrase reflects Brian's all-or-nothing coping style, which intensified when disconnection set in:

- **Attachment Theory** interprets this as an insecure pattern – withdrawal when connection feels unsafe.
- **Social Identity Theory** shows how exclusion from his professional group left him with no partial role to play, only insider or outsider.
- **JD-R and Self-Determination Theory** (introduced earlier in the book) help explain how the lack of autonomy, competence feedback and recognition undermined motivation, pushing Brian towards disengagement rather than sustained effort.

This shows how disconnection often triggers extremes: overinvestment when belonging feels secure, and complete retreat when it is threatened.

"I want to do something that matters"

Despite his disengagement, Brian's longing for meaningful work persisted.

- **Logotherapy** identifies this as the "will to meaning," an intrinsic drive that survives even in despair.
- **Recognition Theory** shows how he sought future roles that would affirm his value and dignity.
- **Social Identity Theory** emphasises the search for new in-groups where his expertise and leadership would be respected.
- **Attachment Theory** frames his eventual mentoring role as an activation of his caregiving system – finding security in supporting others.
- **Ecological Systems Theory** reminds us that this was also shaped by life stage and wider economic forces (chronosystem), which made the question of legacy particularly salient.

Brian's desire to matter was therefore both profoundly personal and socially embedded, reflecting the universal human need for purpose and contribution.

Brian's eventual recovery demonstrates the integrative nature of these theories. Returning to the gym and coaching football provided structure and safe, familiar relationships (Attachment Theory), restored recognition and social esteem (Recognition and Social Identity Theories) and enabled him to reframe his redundancy as an opportunity for growth (Logotherapy). These activities also rebalanced his ecological system, strengthening microsystem connections and creating new, value-aligned pathways.

Together, Brian's words reveal the arc of his disconnection and recovery. *"I feel like I'm disappearing"* captured the erosion of identity, belonging and recognition. *"I'm either all in, or I shut down"* revealed the insecure attachment patterns and extremes of engagement that disconnection triggered. Finally, *"I want to do something that matters"* expressed the enduring human will to meaning, which became the foundation for his recovery.

What Brian's story shows us

Viewed collectively, his words illustrate how disconnection is not just a single experience but a layered breakdown across purpose, safety, recognition and group belonging. Theories help us understand how different dimensions interact, including existential loss (Logotherapy), misrecognition and identity erosion (Recognition and Social Identity Theories), insecure coping (Attachment Theory) and systemic pressures (Ecological Systems Theory). Equally, they highlight the pathways back to achieving meaning and recognition, as well as forging secure relationships and new group identities.

Brian's words remind us that disconnection is never one-dimensional: it erodes meaning, destabilises relationships and fractures identity across multiple layers. As practitioners, his words offer powerful signals to listen for in clients' stories, helping us identify when disconnection is taking hold and which levers of recovery may be most effective. We'll return to these themes at an organisational level in the final chapter.

Decoding and resolving Brian's disconnection tendencies

As Brian's energy lifted, so did his clarity. With the gym routine back in place and time spent coaching the youth football team again, Brian began to feel more like himself. One morning, after a particularly energising session, he said, "I'd forgotten how much I love seeing people grow. It gives me something back."

It was the opening we needed.

In one of our sessions, I invited him to explore what energised him most using Seligman's positive psychology PERMA model, which explores Positive emotion, Engagement, Relationships, Meaning and Accomplishment.

He quickly lit up. "I feel energised when I'm making progress," he said, "when someone else is learning, and we're building something real together."

We added in the VIA character strengths profile and 16 Personalities test to help him rediscover the language for what he already knew deep down. "Leadership, judgement, perseverance," he read aloud. "That's me in a nutshell."

From there, we started connecting dots.

We mapped those strengths onto moments when he had felt most alive at work. Every example he shared had a clear pattern: mentoring early-career professionals, creating clarity in complex projects and helping people move from confusion to confidence. Then he paused, almost surprised.

"I can turn strategy into operational reality," he said. "That's what I'm best at."

It was a lightbulb moment that marked Brian's reconnection with himself and a clear personal sense of purpose.

I asked him one of the questions I return to often: "What difference do you want to make, to whom or what and how specifically?"

He didn't hesitate. "I want to help smart, curious people, maybe younger, earlier in their careers, who don't yet know how good they are. I want to build their confidence and show them how to lead and deliver. No one taught me that."

As a project manager, Brian was used to frameworks. So, when the coaching conversation turned to decision-making, it was not surprising that he decided to create his own mnemonic to use as a simple, acronym-based lens that would guide his choices.

He called it HARP:

- **H**elpful to others;
- Offers real **A**chievement;

- Provides **R**ecognition;
- Connects with a deeper **P**urpose.

"If it doesn't pass the HARP test," he told me later, "I'm not doing it."

As he was used to corporate life, we used a typical business approach to help him clarify what "the right role" looked like, so we could develop a strategy to get him there. As Brian's *HARP* statement reflected his key values, I encouraged him to work on creating a vision, mission and goals statement to accompany *HARP*. Again, he applied his project management experience to create his own *"VMOST"* Career plan, which included the strategy and tactics to achieve it:

- **Vision**: To make a difference through project leadership and mentoring.
- **Mission**: To help others deliver outcomes with clarity and confidence.
- **Objectives**: Paid roles, mentoring, governance and volunteering.
- **Strategy and Tactics**: Trial options, test culture fit, say yes only when *HARP*-aligned.

We explored what "meaningful" felt like on the ground, and what kind of work environment he would need to thrive. He identified that it needed to be structured but human and outcome-focused and collaborative.

At that point in his story a door opened.

A woman he had mentored 25 years earlier reached out. She was now in a senior role at a pharmaceutical consultancy and wanted to recommend him for a leadership position. "You're the first person I thought of," she said.

He soon learnt that the COO knew him from years ago, too. "In 25 years, I've never seen anything better than what we had back then," she said. Suddenly, Brian had an opportunity he was made for.

We worked together to prepare for the interview and final presentation. He had to explain his career story and outline a high-level plan for the department. We used my ASKE model shared previously in Chapter 2 to shape his narrative:

- **Attitude/aptitude:** High-performing achiever with a mentoring mindset.
- **Signature strengths and talents:** Using project management as a framework for growth.
- **Knowledge:** Governance, transformation and people development.
- **Experience:** Sharing real-world stories of trust, turnaround and delivery.

To ground his confidence, I invited him to choose a magic moment when he felt fantastic. He immediately went back to a moment when he had completed a half-marathon after only seven weeks of training.

"There's nowhere to hide on a half-marathon," he said. "The time that showed on my watch was mine. It made me feel unstoppable."

We used this moment as an anchor. I taught him a visualisation exercise to help him embody that strength so he could access it just before the presentation. I encouraged him to describe how it felt and create a short anchor phrase he could use to be in the right state of mind. Brian practised diligently.

"Ready to shine," he whispered to himself as he entered the building.

He got the job.

"It's the right company," he said later. "The people are rock solid. I trust them. It gives me everything I was looking for – challenge, purpose and people who actually value what I bring."

More than that, it gave him a sense of identity and direction. He had been able to reconnect not only with meaningful work, but with himself and with others, so he felt like he belonged and had purpose once again.

*****

Using the ABCDE model to help Brian move forward

Activating event

As we know, Brian's work life began to unravel after he took a senior project management role in a start-up led by a former CEO he had previously trusted. Although initially energised, his remit soon changed to a vague Merger and Acquisition focus in response to business changes. With little to do, long, solitary hours, and no feedback or direction, he began to feel invisible. His formal redundancy, confirmed abruptly by text, further compounded his sense of loss. What hit hardest was not the job itself, but the erosion of identity, connection and rhythm. As Brian said, "I feel like I'm disappearing."

Beliefs

The longer the situation persisted, the more Brian's high-achiever-based beliefs became evident:

- *"If I'm not actively contributing, I'm not valuable."*

- *"I've lost my direction – and maybe I should just retire."*

- *"I don't want to work for people who don't match my standards."*

- *"I'm either all in, or I shut down."*

These beliefs reflected Brian's deeply held values: autonomy, integrity, contribution and competence. These had also created rigidity, especially when his environment no longer supported them.

Consequences

The impact of these beliefs was wide-ranging.

Emotionally, Brian was showing both a persistent low mood and early signs of burnout. Physically, he was sleeping poorly, and his energy levels had dropped significantly. His appetite to look for professional work was flatlining.

Cognitively, his motivation was also diminished, affecting his decision-making and, initially, his aspirations.

Behaviourally, he was changing too, becoming increasingly withdrawn when it came to job search and social interaction.

Socially, he was becoming increasingly isolated, made worse by having had to step away from coaching youth football, which had given him so much pleasure. Finally, when it came to Brian's concept of his own **identity,** he was experiencing a growing disconnection from purpose and professional self-concept, causing him to lose hope.

Dispute

As coaching progressed, these beliefs were gently challenged and re-evaluated. Early work focused on re-establishing wellbeing and reconnection: returning to the gym, rejoining the football community and taking small steps to re-engage. As Brian's energy lifted, so did his clarity and ability to start moving forward again.

A key turning point came through the coaching question I often use with clients:

"What difference do you want to make, to whom or what and how specifically?"

This shifted his internal dialogue and unlocked a new narrative. Brian highlighted mentoring early-career professionals as a meaningful focus and began to explore how his core professional strength, project management, could become a vehicle for contribution.

As a result of our work, Brian applied his love of acronyms to develop his own personal decision-making lens, *HARP*, which represented the key impact values he wanted his future career to represent: **H**elping others, **A**chievement-oriented, **R**ecognition, **P**urposefulness.

Gaining language through the tools we used, VIA Character Strengths and personality tests, enabled him to reflect on and explain both who he is and what matters to him in a positive and supportive way, which helped reset his thinking back to its more normal positive approach. Both PERMA and ASKE provided frameworks he could use to apply that language to and develop into something concrete, an approach he was comfortable with due to his project management background. Supporting him to use his own *VMOST* framework enabled him to create a structured, values-aligned career strategy that he could implement confidently.

When a concrete opportunity emerged, we used the ASKE model to structure his interview preparation, helping him articulate his **A**ttitude, **S**ignature strengths, **K**nowledge and **E**xperience in a compelling narrative. To anchor his confidence for the final presentation, we identified his "magic moment" of completing a half-marathon after only seven weeks of training, and he learnt how to use a visualisation technique to connect with his final effective belief: "I know who I am and what I bring – and I'm ready to shine."

Together, these activities and approaches helped him regain his self-efficacy and start rebuilding his confidence, mindset and future purpose.

Effect

By the time Brian accepted a new leadership role, his internal beliefs had shifted significantly and were now much more like the Brian of old:

- *"I can use project leadership and mentoring to make a difference."*

- *"I work best in places where people share my standards and values."*

- *"If something doesn't pass the HARP test, it's not for me."*

- *"Belonging and purpose are non-negotiables for me to thrive."*

- *"I know who I am and what I bring – and I'm ready to shine."*

These more empowering beliefs supported Brian to move from drift to direction, restoring not just his career purpose, but his sense of identity and connection.

Activities to create changes in disconnection thinking and behaviour

As we saw in Brian's story, one of the primary ways to resolve disconnection is to work at values level. Several of the activities from previous chapters are particularly helpful here, including the Creating a Life Values Compass (Chapter 2) and Achieving Authentically (Chapter 3). The following three activities address disconnection through complementary approaches. Once again, they can be used individually or as a progressive sequence. These activities are designed to enable a client to: understand how environmental systems influence their connection experiences; reflect on their personal connection patterns over time; and identify their group belonging and recognition needs. These activities are informed by key theories from this chapter and designed to support deeper insight, renewed agency and pathways to reconnection.

ACTIVITY 1: MAY THE FIVE FORCES BE WITH YOU: EXPLORING THE ECOLOGICAL SYSTEMS THAT AFFECT CAREERS

This activity uses Bronfenbrenner's Ecological Systems Theory to help clients explore the interrelationships between themselves and their career environment.

Step 1: Understanding the five environmental systems or forces

To pre-frame this activity, you will need to explain that these five interconnected environmental systems come from Bronfenbrenner's Ecological Systems Theory. This model helps clients recognise how their interactions with the five different types of environmental forces shape their career development, wellbeing and sense of connection over time.

- **Microsystem – direct, daily interactions:** The immediate environments you interface with, whether in-person or digitally, including your team, managers, close colleagues, family and friends.
- **Mesosystem – connections between microsystems:** The interplay between your different environments, for example, how stress at work affects your home life or how family needs and expectations shape career choices.
- **Exosystem – indirect influences on you:** Broader systems that affect you without your direct involvement, such as decisions made by senior leaders, policy changes, industry regulations, economic conditions or political disruption.
- **Macrosystem – cultural and societal values:** The overarching beliefs, norms and ideologies that shape all other systems, such as societal expectations and attitudes about career success, cultural and workplace norms, rest, leadership, gender or ambition.
- **Chronosystem – time-driven change:** The life transitions and broader historical or societal shifts that affect you over time, such as career stage transitions, technological disruption, economic recessions or major societal change.

Step 2: Reflection on each force

Now encourage your client to consider each force or system in turn and identify:

- **Positive examples** of times when connection felt strong, supported or meaningful.
- **Negative examples** when they felt disconnected, undervalued or strained.

(Note: If the full exercise feels overwhelming for the client, then focus on the one or two systems or forces that seem most relevant to their current disconnection patterns.)

Step 3: Exploring patterns for insights

Here are some questions you can use to help the client review what they have identified:

- *"Which systems do you find most nourishing or most draining?"*
- *"Where are your strongest sources of support – or stress?"*
- *"What patterns can you identify from this?"*
- *"What themes or surprises do you notice?"*
- *"Which systems could you strengthen or reshape?"*
- *"What's within your influence to reframe, adapt or change?"*
- *"What support do you need from others or from your environment?"*

By broadening their perspective and reducing self-blame, this exercise empowers clients and particularly high achievers to reduce inappropriate self-blame, identify actionable changes and understand the environmental conditions they need to thrive.

ACTIVITY 2: EXPLORING CONNECTION PEAKS AND TROUGHS: MAPPING EMOTIONAL HIGHS AND LOWS

This activity uses narrative techniques to help clients map emotional peaks and troughs in their career timeline. Doing so enables them to surface patterns in belonging, engagement and disconnection and create strategies to sustain connection in future roles.

Setting the scene

Explain to your client that they will be creating a visual timeline of their career journey, focusing specifically on moments of strong connection and disconnection. This approach helps externalise their experience, making patterns more visible and creating distance from overwhelming emotions.

Step 1: Creating the career timeline

Ask your client to create a timeline of their career journey using whatever format feels most natural to them – drawing, writing, arts performance, use of creative kinaesthetic techniques like Lego or storytelling. The timeline should include:

- Key career milestones and transitions.
- Significant work relationships and team experiences.
- Major projects, achievements or challenges.
- Times when they felt most and least connected to their work.

Step 2: Identifying peaks and troughs

Once the timeline is complete, ask your client to identify and mark:

- **Peak experiences:** These are key moments when they felt strongly connected, engaged, valued or like they truly belonged.
- **Trough experiences:** These are key moments when they felt disconnected, isolated, undervalued or disengaged.

Encourage clients to describe how those moments *felt*, not just what happened.

Step 3: Pattern recognition and meaning-making

This step helps them to unpick and use key experiences to create a better future. Here are some questions to help your client explore the patterns in their timeline:

- *"What do you notice about the peaks – what conditions were present when you felt most connected?"*
- *"Were these moments connected to people, purpose, recognition, identity or something else?"*
- *"What patterns do you see in the troughs – what was missing or problematic during disconnected periods?"*
- *"Which experiences feel most significant to your sense of professional identity?"*
- *"What resources, relationships or conditions helped you move from trough experiences back to peaks?"*
- *"What does this timeline tell you about what you need to feel connected and engaged at work?"*

Step 4: Future-focused reflection

Now encourage your client to use their insights to look forward with the following questions:

- *"Based on these patterns, what conditions would you want to create or seek in future roles?"*
- *"What early warning signs might indicate you're moving towards disconnection?"*
- *"What proactive steps could you take to strengthen connection or recover more quickly if disconnection starts to emerge?"*

If you are working with a group, consider inviting participants to share one peak and one trough experience in pairs, using these prompts:

- *"What stands out most from your partner's story?"*
- *"What common themes do you notice across different people's experiences?"*

This activity helps clients externalise their career narrative, identify personal patterns of connection and disconnection from real lived moments, and develop practical strategies for maintaining engagement and belonging in their professional lives.

ACTIVITY 3: RECOGNITION AND BELONGING MAPPING: UNDERSTANDING WHERE YOU FEEL SEEN AND VALUED

This activity uses Social Identity Theory and Recognition Theory to help clients examine their relationships with different groups and identify where they experience authentic belonging and recognition versus conditional acceptance.

Setting the scene

Explaining that recognition and belonging are fundamental human needs that significantly impact workplace engagement and career satisfaction will help the client contextualise this exercise. By mapping their experiences across different groups and relationships, clients will be able to identify their own patterns of connection and disconnection.

Step 1: Taking a group and relationship inventory

Ask your client to list the key groups and relationships in their professional and personal life. These might include:

- **Professional groups:** This includes their current team, department, professional associations, industry networks, and former colleagues.
- **Personal groups:** This covers family, close friends, hobby communities, neighbourhood groups, and volunteer organisations.
- **Hybrid groups:** This means mentoring relationships, alumni networks and social groups that include work contacts.

For each group, ask your client to note their current level of involvement across three options – active, peripheral, inactive.

Step 2: Recognition and belonging assessment (15 minutes)

Now, for each significant group, ask your client to assess their experience using these dimensions and questions:

Recognition: *"How valued and seen do you feel for your authentic contributions in this group?"* (Rate: High/Low)

Belonging: *"How much do you feel you truly fit in and connect with this group?"* (Rate: High/Low)

Encourage your client to consider the following questions:

- *"Do you feel seen for who you really are, or do you need to perform a role?"*
- *"Would this group miss you if you weren't there?"*
- *"Can you be authentic about both strengths and challenges?"*

Step 3: Plotting insights on the recognition and belonging grid

	High belonging	Low belonging
High recognition	Thriving	Performing
Low recognition	Connected but unseen	Disconnectd

To use the grid, encourage your client to place each group into one of four categories in the chart below, using the following category explanations and guidance:

High belonging and high recognition

- **Thriving**: These are your most nourishing groups. You feel both seen and that you belong. Invest in and protect these relationships.

High belonging and low recognition

- **Connected but unseen**: You feel emotionally connected, but your contributions may go unnoticed. Explore how to express your needs or advocate for recognition.

Low belonging and high recognition

- **Performing**: You are valued for what you do but do not feel like you truly fit in. Consider whether a deeper connection is possible or if this environment still serves you.

Low belonging and low recognition

- **Disconnected**: These groups may be draining or misaligned. Consider reducing involvement or reframing your role.

Step 4: Pattern analysis and action planning

The following questions will help your client to examine their grid:

- *"What do you notice about where most of your groups fall?"*
- *"Which quadrant do you want to expand, and which might you want to minimise?"*
- *"What specific conditions in your Thriving quadrant groups could you seek in future relationships?"*
- *"For groups in other quadrants, what one small change might shift the dynamic?"*
- *"How can you become better at creating recognition and belonging for others?"*

If you are working with multiple people, it is worth encouraging participants to share insights about their grid patterns and discuss what conditions help groups move towards the Thriving quadrant.

In summary, using this activity helps clients to understand their relational patterns, distinguish between healthy and unhealthy recognition dynamics, and make conscious choices about where to invest their social and professional energy for greater connection and engagement.

Summary

As Brian's story illustrates, when we can help clients to re-establish a healthy connection to themselves and supportive networks, they become empowered to choose and thrive in purposeful careers that fit, motivate and sustain them. Where disconnection occurs, whether from self, others or meaningful purpose, however, it can lead clients to consider career choices that lack fulfilment, increase risk of disengagement or lead to frequent change and uncertainty, as we saw in Brian's case. When we are disconnected from ourselves, others and purpose, it provides the perfect context for our seventh and final thief to strike – the Thief of Burnout, as the next chapter shows.

6. The Thief of Disconnection
At a glance

Working definition: "A psychological state in which individuals experience a profound sense of detachment from meaning, recognition, and their authentic selves. This state often leads to emotional withdrawal and reduced engagement with work and life."

Key theories and models:

1. **Logotherapy (Frankl, 1946/1959):** Psychological distress stems from loss of meaning. When individuals cannot connect work or life to a deeper purpose, they experience the "existential vacuum."
2. **Recognition Theory (Honneth, 1992):** Self-worth develops through being seen, valued and affirmed. When recognition is denied across personal, legal or social spheres, disconnection occurs.

Impact and context:

Leading predictor of disengagement, presenteeism, "quiet quitting"; only 10% of UK employees are fully engaged.

Costs $438 billion globally in lost productivity; particularly impacts high achievers who define themselves through contribution.

Women feel disconnection as exclusion/isolation; men may withdraw emotionally or avoid seeking support.

High in remote/tech sectors, competitive environments; lower in collaborative mission-driven organisations.

- **Early career:** Lack of purpose/misalignment.
- **Mid-career:** Values conflicts.
- **Late career:** Loss of role/status.

Warning signs:

- **Identity loss:** "I feel like I'm disappearing."
- **Meaning vacuum:** Work and life feel pointless or hollow.
- **Emotional withdrawal:** Reduced investment in relationships and activities.
- **Quiet quitting:** Doing the minimum required, avoiding extra engagement.
- **Values misalignment:** Daily actions conflict with core beliefs.
- **Social isolation:** Withdrawing from colleagues and communities.
- **Existential questioning:** "What's the point of all this?"

When connection and purpose are lost

3. **Attachment Theory (Bowlby, 1969, Ainsworth, 1978; Hasan and Shaver, 1987):** Early bonding patterns shape emotional regulation and workplace connection. Insecure attachment increases the risk of disconnection through relational avoidance.
4. **Social Identity Theory (Tajfel and Turner, 1979):** Self-esteem and belonging depend on group membership. Threats to identity from exclusion or marginalisation can lead to disconnection and withdrawal.
5. **Ecological Systems Theory (Bronfenbrenner, 1979):** Disconnection arises from misalignment across nested systems: individual, relational, organisational, cultural, highlighting how context shapes engagement.

Neuroscience:

Disconnection creates measurable changes in brain function and chemistry, affecting how we relate to others and ourselves:

- **Social brain networks:** Reduced activity in medial PFC and posterior cingulate cortex.
- **Threat detection:** Amygdala becomes hyperactive, interpreting exclusion as danger.
- **Oxytocin decline:** Reduced bonding hormone makes trust and connection difficult.
- **Dopamine depletion:** Decreased motivation and reduced sense of reward from activities.

Chronic disconnection triggers the same neural pathways as physical pain, explaining why social rejection feels genuinely painful and requires safety-building first.

Key coaching activities:

1. **Five Forces Analysis:** Use Bronfenbrenner's ecological systems to explore how environmental forces affect career connection and engagement.
2. **Connection Timeline Mapping:** Identify peaks and troughs in belonging to understand personal patterns and conditions for meaningful engagement.
3. **Recognition and Belonging Grid:** Map relationships across high/low recognition and belonging dimensions to identify thriving versus disconnected groups.

Core takeaway: Shift from **isolation** to **meaningful connection**.

7 | The Thief of Burnout

Self-neglect through constantly prioritising work over wellbeing

> "In the midst of darkness, light persists."
>
> Mahatma Gandhi, Indian lawyer, politician, social activist and writer.

Anwen's story

Anwen was already off sick when we started working together in the autumn. In her late 40s, she had been a university lecturer for more than two decades.

On paper, she had a solid career: permanent post, decent income, academic freedom and a reputation for reliability. Research deadlines, lectures and student support were once sources of energy and pride. However, the institution had changed – and so had she.

Everything now felt performative, transactional. Intellectual curiosity was buried beneath an avalanche of admin, clunky systems and relentless student demands. "I used to love seeing the light come on for a student," she said. "But now... they want to be spoon-fed. And I'm the one who's starving."

Loyal, bright and deeply committed, her energy was gone – she was not just tired, she was totally and persistently depleted. What started with COVID led to a series of infections that left her with post-viral fatigue. Days blurred together: too weak to concentrate, too foggy to read, even the kitchen some mornings felt out of reach. And yet, her mind wouldn't stop spinning.

"It's not just the illness," she said quietly. "It's the job. It's all of it."

She described her work as a treadmill that kept running whether you stood on it or not. Exhausted physically and emotionally, she was still unsure whether what she was feeling was burnout or simply weakness. We explored the difference together to help her identify that burnout is not a failure of resilience; it is the body's protest against sustained, values-violating overload.

We began by creating a safe landing place. I introduced simple mindfulness tools, including grounding breath and orienting practices, to calm her nervous system. Like many high-functioning professionals, Anwen had become so used to overriding her body that she'd stopped hearing it scream. Her reaction was immediate. "It makes me feel present again," she admitted. I suggested that these tools could quieten the stress response and allow her to start rebuilding reserves. We also discussed the importance of self-compassion so she could treat herself with the same kindness she offered to others. I signposted her to meditation apps to help her practise.

She responded well and began to track her energy more consciously, noticing how even small social interactions could drain her for days. That clarity became foundational. "My body," she said, "has started dictating the terms of engagement – and it's doing a better job than I ever did."

From there, we began to unpick her story gently and carefully.

We returned to her values. She listed fairness, calm, depth and contribution. I asked her what she most wanted from work and what pushed her too far. At first, she struggled: her job description was so broad it could encompass almost anything. But slowly the truth emerged.

Using the Life Values Compass (see Chapter 2), she mapped what mattered most: meaningful connection, autonomy, deep work and integrity. The contrast with her daily reality was stark: she craved focus but lived in chaos; she wanted fairness but felt exploited; she valued autonomy but endured micro-management; she loved depth but was forced into surface-level tasks.

When we discussed the possibility of a more research-focused role, she paused. It no longer felt like a solution, just a reshuffling of the same deck. The gap between her values and the work demanded of her had become unbridgeable. "I don't like it, and it has made me ill," she said. It was clear that naming it was liberating.

"I think I've been trying to serve everyone except myself," she confessed, tears welling up. "And the cost of that… well, it's me. I don't want to go back. Not even for the parts I loved. I'm not ready for what comes next. But I know it's not this."

She needed permission to stop. For someone as principled as Anwen, however, this was not a simple matter. Her identity was entwined with her job. Leaving felt like betrayal. She wrestled with guilt about colleagues and with the pressure to "push through." Together, we discussed the distinction between self-sacrifice and self-neglect. We reframed "quitting" as choosing a different kind of service, one rooted in sustainability rather than martyrdom.

"I've only ever had one job," she said. "It feels like a prison sentence. But I didn't realise I could leave. That surprised me."

That was the turning point and a decision made not from certainty, but from survival.

She needed space to recover and rest, so I suggested we pause the coaching. Her only task was to practise the breathing and orienting techniques – and, if she felt able, to dip into my book, *Change Your Story*, at her own pace. "Your job," I told her, "is to stop making yourself the machine."

*****

So, what is burnout?

The World Health Organisation defines burnout as *"a syndrome conceptualized as resulting from chronic workplace stress that has not been successfully managed. It is characterized by three dimensions: feelings of energy depletion or exhaustion; increased mental distance from one's job, or feelings of negativism or cynicism related to one's job; and reduced professional efficacy."* Although the WHO definition states that *"burnout refers specifically to phenomena in the occupational context and should not be applied to describe experiences in other areas of life,"* there is growing research-based evidence that it is now seen to spread beyond purely a work context.

Similar exhaustion–cynicism–inefficacy patterns are found in caregiving, parenting, academic study, chronic illness management, financial strain, community or volunteer roles and even digital overload or relationship conflict. In these contexts, the mechanism is the same: prolonged, unrelieved stress without sufficient recovery leads to depletion, detachment and loss of efficacy.

From a personality perspective, burnout is closely associated with several traits from the OCEAN/Big Five model:

High Neuroticism, characterised by anxiety, emotional instability and susceptibility to stress, consistently predicts higher risk across all three dimensions of burnout: emotional exhaustion, depersonalisation and reduced personal accomplishment.

Low Conscientiousness is also a significant predictor, reflecting weaker goal management and stress-coping capacity, whereas **higher Conscientiousness** is generally protective.

Lower Extraversion (introversion, withdrawal, reduced reliance on social networks) may increase vulnerability by limiting access to social support, though the effect varies by context.

Findings for **Agreeableness** are mixed: very low scores can hinder relationship support, while very high scores may predispose individuals to overcommitment and difficulty setting boundaries; overall, moderate to higher scores tend to be somewhat protective, particularly against depersonalisation.

Openness to experience shows the least consistent relationship with burnout: some studies link lower Openness to less adaptive coping, while others find little or no effect, with results varying depending on how Openness is measured.

Other constructs also play a role:

- **Perfectionists** often set unattainably high standards, leading to chronic dissatisfaction and exhaustion.
- **People-pleasers**, highly attuned to others' approval and low in assertiveness, may overcommit and neglect their own limits.
- **Workaholics**, driven by compulsive or excessive work patterns, are at high risk if these behaviours go unchecked.
- Individuals with a **high need for achievement (nAch)** can experience both protection and risk. Where environments provide recognition, resources and achievable goals, nAch can drive energy and resilience. But when persistent obstacles, poor feedback or unrealistic demands block achievement, the same drive fuels frustration, exhaustion and eventually burnout. For high achievers, the relentless pursuit of goals without boundaries or self-care can turn ambition into self-neglect.

The Maslach Burnout Inventory (MBI) is recognised as the gold standard self-administered test to assess levels of burnout across three core dimensions – emotional exhaustion, depersonalisation and personal accomplishment.

Why should we be worried about burnout?

Burnout can cause exhaustion, mental health risks, job dissatisfaction and damaged relationships. From a health perspective, burnout is characterised by chronic fatigue, sleep disturbances, frequent headaches, muscle pain, gastrointestinal issues and reduced immunity, all of which are often linked to stress.

The second Annual Burnout Report 2025 by Mental Health UK reveals a growing generational divide in workplace stress levels, with 34% of adults experiencing high or extreme levels of pressure or stress in 2024. Nine in ten experienced high pressure or stress at some point over the last year. Individuals aged 18–24 are most likely to be absent due to poor mental health caused by stress, and a decline in their likelihood to open up with line managers about stress levels. Interventions such as reasonable adjustments, mental health training and a supportive line manager can help alleviate stress and prevent burnout. The report also highlights gaps in healthcare, with 18–24-year-olds three times more likely to need time off due to deteriorating health caused by NHS delays than those aged 55+.

In the **workplace**, burnout can lead to emotional, behavioural, cognitive and physical symptoms, undermining both individual performance and the wider work environment. Individuals often present with chronic exhaustion, low energy, irritability, low motivation, withdrawal and isolation, as well as frequent physical issues such as fatigue, headaches and sleep disturbance. Cognitive symptoms are equally important, with many individuals experiencing difficulties with concentration, cynicism and self-doubt. In response, some individuals attempt to overcompensate by working longer hours, which only deepens exhaustion and disengagement, ultimately eroding productivity.

According to the UK Health and Safety Executive (HSE), in 2023–4, an estimated 33.7 million working days were lost due to work-related ill health and injury, of which 16.4 million days (49%) were the result of stress, depression or anxiety. Workers affected by these conditions took an average of 21.1 days off, compared with 14.3 days for musculoskeletal disorders, which themselves accounted for 7.8 million lost days.

The rise of digital and hybrid working has introduced new risks, including "always-on" expectations, blurred work-life boundaries, increased screen fatigue and social isolation from reduced face-to-face interaction. At the same time, the loss of natural transition rituals, such as commuting, has made it harder to separate work from personal life.

Burnout also has significant team-level impacts. It reduces productivity, quality and innovation, while undermining collaboration and increasing absenteeism. These effects often spread, leading to collective disengagement, loss of enthusiasm and reduced investment in tasks. Ultimately, burnout can drive talented individuals to leave altogether, depriving organisations of their top performers and weakening workplace wellbeing.

In **education**, burnout has a significant impact, negatively affecting both students and educators. High levels of burnout in students are associated with decreased academic performance, reduced learning satisfaction and increased absenteeism. Burnout symptoms also predict dropouts and absenteeism, as stress accumulates over time.

When it comes to teachers, the 2024 Teacher Wellbeing Index shows persistently high rates of stress, anxiety, depression and burnout, with 77% of all staff experiencing symptoms of poor mental health due to work, and 46% experiencing insomnia or difficulty sleeping. Factors contributing to burnout include perceived lack of support, excessive workload and insufficient resources. High burnout can lead to emotional exhaustion, cynicism and a decrease in job satisfaction. It can also affect mental health, school climate, student outcomes and overall school functioning. The picture is equally challenging in further and higher education, with significant numbers considering leaving the sector every year. Positive values, supportive leadership and healthy work-life integration can help reduce the risk of burnout and improve outcomes for both students and teachers.

From an **age** perspective, burnout is a common issue among young and early-career workers, with the highest levels in the first years of a career. As workers age, burnout risk decreases, with some studies showing an increase for those over 55 due to new life and work challenges. Burnout disproportionately affects students and new graduates, particularly Millennials and Gen Z, due to high workloads, work-life balance, job insecurity and blurred boundaries between work and personal life.

Gender plays a significant role in burnout, with women reporting higher rates due to emotional exhaustion and workforce inequalities. Men are more likely to experience depersonalisation, while women feel emotionally drained. Burnout risk in women peaks in early-career years and after around age 55, while for men the risk generally decreases as they age. The gender-burnout link is intensified in traditionally female-dominated sectors. Once again, having effective support systems in place can buffer this risk.

Neurodivergent individuals, including those with autism, ADHD and dyslexia, are at a significantly higher risk for burnout compared to neurotypical peers. Research shows that neurodivergent individuals report higher rates of burnout, often due to the continuous effort to suppress natural ways of thinking and behaving to conform to neurotypical expectations. Burnout symptoms include severe fatigue, increased sensory sensitivity, executive function breakdown, social withdrawal, diminished coping skills and sometimes loss of previously acquired skills. Environmental mismatch, lack of understanding, reasonable accommodations and supportive management are key environmental factors. Difficulties in self-organisation, time management and attention also contribute to burnout. Life impact includes loss of function, increased anxiety, depression, impaired work ability, increased unemployment risk and reduced quality of life.

Socio-economic status (SES) also plays an important part in the likelihood of burnout, with individuals with lower SES at greater risk. Factors contributing to this include lower household income, lower education levels, limited training and early-career opportunities, low job satisfaction and a persistent economic impact. Economic stress amplifies work stress, making those with financial strain, fewer resources and a limited workplace voice more vulnerable, as theories such as the Conservation of Resources and the Job-Demands-Resources model have identified.

Finally, from a **cultural and ethnicity perspective**, burnout rates vary significantly and are shaped by national cultural traits, workplace environments and broader social contexts. Dimensions such as high power distance, high masculinity and high uncertainty avoidance are linked to higher burnout. At the same time, individualistic Western countries often report more overt symptoms, while collectivist or hierarchical societies may experience more internalised stress with less open expression. In the UK, for instance, burnout is strongly influenced by social expectations, workplace conditions, discrimination and systemic inequalities. Black, Asian, and Minority Ethnic (BAME) professionals, particularly in high-stress sectors, report higher burnout rates than their White British counterparts, often due to discrimination, underrepresentation in senior roles, insecure employment, lower pay and limited access to support.

Yet, international studies also suggest that some minority groups, such as Asian, Black and Hispanic/Latinx physicians, can report lower odds of burnout, reflecting the protective effects of stronger social support and distinct coping strategies. Overall, this highlights that social determinants, workplace policies and support networks are more critical than ethnicity alone. Addressing burnout effectively requires tackling structural inequalities, embedding inclusive and culturally sensitive interventions, and reshaping organisational systems to provide equitable conditions for wellbeing and progression. While burnout often has a clear negative impact on an individual's progression, as we have seen in Anwen's case, it can also motivate change, prompting self-reflection, seeking help and advocating for better work conditions and support systems.

Burnout and sectors

Widespread across the UK workforce, its form and severity vary by sector. Certain roles are particularly vulnerable due to structural demands, emotional labour, and cultural pressures:

- **Healthcare and NHS:** Among the highest rates, with ambulance and clinical staff most affected. Understaffing, long shifts and high caseloads drive exhaustion and high turnover.
- **Education:** Multiple surveys indicate that up to 75% of teachers report persistent stress, fuelled by workload, accountability demands and poor work-life balance, with primary and nursery teachers especially at risk.
- **Police, social work and welfare:** Here, stress levels are well above the national average, linked to trauma exposure, emotional demand and excessive caseloads.
- **Hospitality, finance and tech:** Elevated burnout risk in these sectors stems from unpredictable hours, customer pressures, performance targets and "always-on" cultures.

While burnout is highly prevalent in people-facing public service roles, it also extends across private sector industries where performance and customer demands are paramount.

Burnout among **entrepreneurs** is also a significant issue. In the UK, over one in three business owners and entrepreneurs report severe burnout and mental health issues, such as stress, anxiety, depression and sleep disruption. Many work 48 hours/week or more, with variable schedules, and 80% continue to work when ill due to business demands. Over half of UK founders reported experiencing burnout in the last year, with three-quarters admitting to high levels of anxiety. Risk factors include long hours, role overload, financial pressures due not least to economic and political uncertainty and isolation. Passion for thier business can also serve as a double-edged sword, which both drives business success and can also lead to overwork, perfectionism and neglect of self-care, making burnout more likely. This often creates a physical and emotional toll, strained relationships, reduced decision-making ability and threats to business sustainability. It is also worth remembering that most entrepreneurs receive no sick pay, resulting in working through illness and without sufficient recovery time.

Burnout across the career lifespan

Burnout poses a significant threat to career longevity and sustainability. It undermines professional satisfaction, health and growth. It often accelerates workforce exit, early retirement and lost opportunities, which limit both potential and development, especially when unaddressed. Recognising these patterns highlights the importance of early intervention and ongoing support to sustain careers over the long term:

Early careers: Burnout at this stage can quickly erode an individual's intent to stay in a profession, leading to career disruption, role changes or early exits. They can exhibit quiet quitting behaviours such as doing the minimum required rather than going the extra mile, avoiding extra responsibilities and stepping back emotionally. Although some individuals develop resilience in response, without proper support, the dominant trend is shortened career spans.

Mid-careers: Sustained burnout reduces organisational commitment, willingness to take on responsibility, and reduces the desire to seek promotion, including leadership opportunities. Professionals report stalled advancement, career regret and a higher likelihood of leaving demanding fields such as healthcare, education and social care.

Late careers and retirement: Chronic burnout contributes to poorer physical and psychological health, diminished quality of life and earlier retirement as a means of reducing stress. For some, disengagement outweighs the rewards of continuing, resulting in shortened professional lifespans.

Careers, potential and engagement can be preserved and developed if timely, stage-specific interventions are used to help individuals recover, remain engaged and sustain fulfilling careers.

Burnout often serves as a powerful inflection point in a person's career, forcing deep reflection on values, purpose and long-term goals, and frequently prompting redirection or even major transformation (see previous chapters for related activities). Unfulfilled achievers who experience burnout often move away from external markers of success such as salary or promotion, and instead prioritise intrinsic rewards, including meaning, wellbeing, autonomy and alignment with personal values. For some, this leads to a career pivot where they continue doing the same work in a better environment or sector, or a complete change of direction in search of healthier, more aligned and fulfilling work. Others focus on boundary-setting, negotiating flexible terms or choosing part-time or freelance options to prevent recurrence. Burnout recovery can also spark new professional growth, with individuals retraining, building resilience or even becoming advocates for workplace wellbeing, shaping organisational culture through leadership, mentoring or coaching. At the same time, some choose to downshift or exit high-pressure roles altogether, reducing hours, turning down promotions or retiring early to safeguard health and relationships. In each case, burnout reshapes career direction by redefining success and motivating change, with the ultimate goal of restoring and preserving long-term wellbeing.

The neuroscience of burnout

Burnout is not simply the result of "too much stress." Neuroscience research indicates that it produces distinct, measurable changes in the brain that alter how we think, feel and function. Prolonged exposure to chronic workplace stress can reshape both brain structure and chemistry, explaining why burnout symptoms are so persistent and wide-ranging.

From a structural perspective, the **prefrontal cortex**, responsible for decision-making, self-regulation and working memory, shows reduced activity and potential structural changes, weakening the brain's ability to concentrate, regulate behaviour and manage competing demands. At the same time, the **amygdala**, the brain's alarm system, becomes hyperactive, leading to increased emotional reactivity, heightened vigilance and heightened anxiety. The **hippocampus**, which is crucial for learning and memory, also exhibits signs of atrophy, making it more difficult to retain information and adapt to new challenges.

Brain chemistry

Burnout also disrupts the body's stress-regulation system, the **hypothalamic–pituitary–adrenal (HPA) axis**, the body's primary stress-response system, which acts as our internal alarm and recovery system. The early stages are often marked by high levels of **cortisol**, the primary stress hormone. In later stages, however, the system can become depleted, producing abnormally low cortisol levels. This shift weakens resilience, lowers immunity and increases vulnerability to illness. Neurochemical imbalances in **dopamine**, **serotonin** and **noradrenaline** reduce motivation, impair mood regulation and strip away the normal capacity to experience pleasure. Levels of **brain-derived neurotrophic factor** (BDNF), which supports neuron growth and repair, also fall, reducing the brain's ability to recover from stress.

Chronic stress and burnout increase **pro-inflammatory cytokines**, the chemical "call to action" messengers that our immune systems release to trigger inflammation in the brain, processes associated with depression, cognitive decline and heightened risk of chronic disease. The combined effect is a brain caught in a cycle of impaired cognitive control, heightened threat sensitivity and depleted energy. Clients often describe this as constant fatigue, difficulty concentrating, emotional volatility and loss of enjoyment in activities that once motivated them, all of which align with these neurological changes.

The neuroscience of burnout also presents differently in **neurodivergent individuals**. While both neurotypical and neurodivergent people experience changes in executive function, stress regulation and emotional control, autism and ADHD bring additional vulnerabilities. For example, autistic individuals may already process sensory and emotional input more intensely, so a hyperactive **amygdala** amplifies distress. Those with ADHD often have dopamine regulation differences, meaning the motivational and attentional impacts of burnout can be more severe. In both groups, the sustained effort to mask or adapt to neurotypical expectations adds further strain, accelerating the neurological effect of burnout and increasing the risk of long-term exhaustion. Burnout also affects those with specific learning differences such as dyslexia, dyscalculia and dyspraxia more intensely, too. These individuals often face heightened cognitive load, stigma and a lack of accommodations in the workplace. The extra effort required to mask or compensate can contribute to faster depletion and greater vulnerability to burnout if support systems are absent.

Understanding these neurological underpinnings for any achiever struggling with burnout helps to explain why recovery is a gradual process and why interventions must address both the cognitive and biological aspects of stress.

Burnout theory in action

Anwen's story demonstrates how burnout develops when prolonged effort, misalignment and self-neglect gradually drain energy and meaning. Using Anwen's words as our anchor, we can see how five major burnout models, frameworks and theories collectively illuminate her journey.

"I used to love seeing the light come on for a student. But now... they want to be spoon-fed. And I'm the one who's starving"

This captures the hollowing out of once-joyful work:

- **Maslach et al.'s Three-Dimensional Model** highlights the classic pattern: emotional exhaustion from constant giving, depersonalisation through cynicism towards students and a fading sense of accomplishment.
- **Leiter and Maslach's Areas of Worklife Model** shows misfits across workload, values and fairness: Anwen gave more than she received, her values of curiosity and independence clashed with student expectations and the effort-reward balance collapsed.

"It's not just the illness. It's the job. It's all of it"

Burnout rarely comes from one source; here, Anwen's illness interacted with a draining work environment:

- **Karasek's Demand–Control–Support Model** reveals the imbalance: high teaching and admin demands, limited control over curriculum and workload and insufficient collegial support. This high-strain profile intensified stress and fatigue.
- **Areas of Worklife** reinforces that burnout deepens when misfit accumulates across several domains at once: workload, control, community and values.

"I think I've been trying to serve everyone except myself. And the cost of that... well, it's me"

This insight shows the hidden dynamic of self-neglect at the heart of burnout:

- **Siegrist's Effort-Reward Imbalance (ERI) Model** explains the toxic combination: extreme effort, little recognition and overcommitment fuelled by internalised duty.
- **Maslach's framework** reminds us that this is not weakness but the predictable outcome of systemic imbalance. Burnout is the signal that the system, not the person, is unsustainable.

"I've only ever had one job. It feels like a prison sentence"

Here, burnout shows up as a crisis of identity and meaning.

- **Pines' Existential Theory of Burnout** interprets exhaustion as the collapse of purpose. When roles that once provided meaning no longer do, energy drains away and identity feels imprisoned or lost.

This explains Anwen's grief: not just over illness or workload, but over the disintegration of a career she once defined herself by.

"For the first time in years, I'm not abandoning myself to keep everyone else comfortable"

This marks the beginning of recovery, when Anwen shifted from self-betrayal to self-acknowledgement.

- **The Three Dimensional Model** and the **Areas of Worklife framework** suggest that renewal requires rebalancing mismatched domains, especially values and fairness, so the individual's needs and the role are no longer in conflict.
- **The ERI model** highlights the importance of reducing overcommitment: recovery begins when effort is no longer continually poured into unrewarding contexts.

- **The Existential Theory of Burnout** frames this as a re-emergence of authentic meaning and a move from depletion to self-congruence.

In the next section, we will explore how coaching helped Anwen acknowledge her body's wisdom, challenge the pull of self-neglect and begin rebuilding a career grounded in authenticity and sustainability.

Decoding and resolving burnout tendencies

When we met again six weeks later, something had shifted. Anwen had applied for a senior advisory role that she was well-suited for, but experienced a chaotic sequence of emails: first rejected, then shortlisted, then rejected again. Instead of destabilising her, it brought clarity. "It feels like a shambles I'm better off avoiding," she said.

She had mentioned her love of painting, so I encouraged her to start using her art to record which activities restored her and which depleted her. At first, short sketches; then, after 18 months of silence, she was painting freely again. "There's been some brain unblocker," she said, laughing. Painting gave her a sense of expression, voice and purpose, even without an audience.

I observed that none of the activities she enjoyed were linked to her university role. "I don't think this is just burnout," I suggested gently. "Could it feel more like a fear of returning to work?" She paused, then nodded. "Yes. That's exactly it. And I didn't see it until you said it."

Together, we explored her working style to name what suited her and what didn't. She valued deep focus, structure and space for intuitive problem-solving. "I'm not a template-follower," she said. "I'm more of a 'what's needed here?' person."

A personality test gave her language to reinforce what she already sensed – that she is responsible, grounded, methodical and enjoys quiet creativity. It reassured her that she did not need to change herself. She simply needed to find an environment that valued her.

Slowly, recovery came. She practised her grounding exercises daily and built a simple routine: tea, completing a daily body scan practice to tune in better internally, and a short journal entry. It was not a lot, but it marked the shift from collapse to agency.

We began exploring the future not as a five-year plan but as a series of small experiments. Ideas included researching and writing about her interest in painting, tutoring, gardening, cooking, volunteering and teaching practical life skills such as basic mending, cooking, budgeting and storytelling. What was emerging was a desire to do something socially useful, hands-on and real.

She smiled as she imagined it. "Working individually within a collective," she said. "Everyone is doing their own thing, but with a shared spirit. That would suit me."

Her reflections sharpened her clarity. Comparing her old department with another she had once collaborated with, she remembered being greeted as a valued colleague rather than a burden. Her body had known long before her mind: the environment she worked in had become toxic.

By March, she had made up her mind. She would resign. By the end of May, the letter was in. "It's absolutely the right decision," she wrote. "Despite some qualms about giving up the parts I did love, I'm realising how long I've hated it."

Anwen was not rushing into something new. She was fortunate to have savings and a supportive partner so she could give herself permission to pause. "I'm not planning a new career just yet – largely because I can't. But I'm doing loads of painting and other projects – and gardening. And I'm going to a local allotment. It's a delight to see what thrives unexpectedly."

This and other experiments supported her as she sought to rediscover herself. She called it her "middle-aged person's gap year." She chose to listen to her body, to honour the wisdom of depletion, and to reject systems that reward endurance over wellbeing.

Now there was no rush, nothing to prove, no hamster wheel. All she had to do was breathe, maintain space and let something meaningful grow, just as the plants in the allotment did.

Her recovery is ongoing. Some days are still hard. However, she no longer views her burnout as a failure. She sees it as a line in the sand. "For the first time in years," she said, "I'm not abandoning myself to keep everyone else comfortable. And that's the kind of career move I wish I'd made a decade ago."

*****

Using the ABCDE model to help Anwen move forward

Activating event

Anwen, a senior lecturer, experienced post-viral fatigue after COVID alongside an academic environment that had become transactional, bureaucratic and values-violating. Once energised by teaching and research, she now felt trapped on a treadmill that drained her completely. As she put it: "I used to love seeing the light come on for a student, but now... they want to be spoon-fed. And I'm the one who's starving."

Beliefs

Anwen had several unhelpful beliefs driving her burnout, including:

- *"If I stop, I'll be betraying my colleagues."*

- *"I've only ever had one job, so I can't leave – it feels like a prison sentence."*

- *"Not pushing through means I'm weak."*

- *"I must serve others even if it costs me."*

As Anwen reflected, "I think I've been trying to serve everyone except myself. And the cost of that... well, it's me."

Consequences

These beliefs created shame, hopelessness, brain fog and physical incapacity. She ignored her body's signals, overrode exhaustion and became trapped in cycles of depletion, reinforcing her sense of being stuck. "It's not just the illness," she said. "It's the job. It's all of it."

Dispute

Coaching reframed burnout as the body's wisdom, not weakness. Using the Life Values Compass, mindfulness, journalling and personality assessment, she recognised the gap between her values and her reality. Small experiments (gardening, painting, journalling, volunteering) allowed her to imagine alternatives and reduce pressure to "have it all figured out." As she discovered: "My body has started dictating the terms of engagement – and it's doing a better job than I ever did."

Effect

- *"Burnout is my body's wisdom, not my weakness."*

- *"Leaving is not failure – it is choosing sustainability."*

- *"My values are a compass for future work."*

- *"Rest and recovery are necessary, not indulgent."*

- *"I don't have to sacrifice myself to be of service."*

Outcome

Anwen resigned, reframing her transition as a "middle-aged person's gap year." She now honours the wisdom of depletion, listens to her body and is allowing a meaningful future to emerge at its own pace. "For the first time in years, I'm not abandoning myself to keep everyone else comfortable. And that's the kind of career move I wish I'd made a decade ago."

Activities to create changes in burnout thinking and behaviour

As the pace and complexity of the working world accelerate, so too does the need for us as career development, education, coaching and HR practitioners to strengthen our capacity to support clients who are experiencing burnout and values misalignment. Career wellbeing, defined by the University of North Georgia as *"the ability to achieve balance between work and leisure time in a manner that provides personal satisfaction that aligns with your values, goals, and lifestyle,"* requires intentional cultivation. By helping our clients and ourselves achieve this alignment, we can foster sustainable careers that provide both professional contribution and consistent personal satisfaction. The following activities are designed to help you do so. As with all activities in this book, use professional judgement and discontinue if clients become distressed and consider whether the client needs to be referred to a suitably qualified medical expert/therapist.

ACTIVITY 1: MANAGING YOUR INNER DOG: AN EXERCISE IN INWARD LISTENING

This exercise helps clients recognise their stress patterns and understand how their body responds to different workplace and life situations. By identifying these patterns, clients become better equipped to recognise early warning signs and learn practical tools to stay calm and focused.

Based on Stephen Porges' **polyvagal theory**, this approach uses simple metaphors to explore physiological and emotional states that correspond to different levels of nervous system activation.

Here is an explanation you can share with clients to help them understand the two main divisions of the peripheral nervous system:

- The **somatic nervous system** governs what we can consciously sense and do (e.g. moving muscles, noticing sensations).
- The **autonomic nervous system** runs automatically in the background, regulates breathing, heart rate, digestion and other life-sustaining processes, (though breathing can also be consciously influenced).

The autonomic nervous system has two primary branches, **sympathetic** and **parasympathetic**. The parasympathetic branch contains two distinct vagal pathways (ventral vagal and dorsal vagal), which means the autonomic system can create three different functional states that shape everyday experiences:

Parasympathetic nervous system (two pathways):

- The **"Rest and digest" or "Safe and connected" state (ventral vagal pathway):** this is active when we feel safe, valued and supported. It underpins recovery, social connection and clear thinking. We'll call this state *Happy Dog*, wagging its tail, energised and ready to engage.

- **The "Shutdown state" (dorsal vagal pathway):** when threats feel inescapable and fight or flight responses aren't viable, the nervous system may shift into protective immobilisation. In this state of hypo-arousal, clients may feel flat, disconnected or "running on empty." We'll call this *Numb Dog*, a dog which is curled up in its bed, too exhausted to wag or bark.

Sympathetic nervous system

- **"Fight or flight state":** this state of negative hyper-arousal is activated when we perceive threat or pressure, whether from overwhelming demands, conflict or lack of support. It mobilises energy for action but, if prolonged, leaves us depleted. We'll call this state *Snappy Dog*, a dog which is restless, reactive and barking at everything.

Step 1: Explore two contrasting experiences

Ask the client to identify two recent workplace moments:

- one where they felt energised, calm or positive (*Happy Dog*);
- one where they felt tense, reactive or overwhelmed (*Snappy Dog*).

If relevant, you may also ask whether they have experienced moments of withdrawal, numbness or flatness (*Numb Dog*).

(Note: encourage clients to choose everyday situations, not catastrophic or traumatic events, so the exercise remains safe and constructive.)

Step 2: Happy Dog exploration

Guide the client through recalling their positive experience. Here are some useful prompts:

- *"What did your body feel like, your breathing, muscle tension, energy levels, posture?"*
- *"What were you thinking and saying to yourself?"*
- *"What emotions were present? How intense were they?"*

Encourage them to note their reflections.

Step 3: Snappy Dog exploration

Repeat the same process for their stressful experience, using the same prompts to help them understand what caused them to become dysregulated.

Step 4: State comparison

Invite the client to compare the two (or three) states using the following questions:

- *"What specific triggers preceded each?"*
- *"What body signals could act as early warning signs?"*
- *"Where else do you notice these patterns in your work or personal life?"*

Step 5: Values and beliefs evaluation

Ask the client to identify which underlying values or beliefs were being respected in the Happy Dog state and which were being violated in the Snappy Dog (and/or Numb Dog) state. This helps reveal workplace conditions that support, rather than undermine wellbeing and provides direction for developing effective regulation strategies. Now that they are conscious about what triggers them, it is the appropriate moment to coach them to choose more effective behavioural responses, which they can test after the session. A reminder of their Happy Dog state at the end of the activity will ensure that the session ends without the client feeling activated.

Helping clients recognise which "inner dog" is present builds foundational awareness for recognising and managing stress.

ACTIVITY 2: INCREASING OUR EMOTIONAL BANDWIDTH: USING THE WINDOW OF TOLERANCE TO STAY BALANCED AND LEARNING FOR LONGER

This activity works well as a standalone exercise or as a follow-on to help clients rebalance, centre and open up to learning. It introduces the concept of the Window of Tolerance and provides two nervous system regulation techniques that can be practised in-session and used independently by clients.

Developed by Dr Dan Siegel, the Window of Tolerance describes the optimal state in which we can manage emotions, continue to learn, and connect with others. When we are within this window, everyday challenges feel manageable. Trauma or prolonged stress can narrow the window, meaning even small triggers may push someone into either:

- Hyper-arousal (anxiety, anger, agitation), or
- Hypo-arousal (numbness, withdrawal, shutdown).

Helping clients understand this concept provides them with a shared language for their experiences and opens the door to practical strategies that enhance their capacity for regulation and resilience.

The image below shows the Window of Tolerance and maps the positions of the different types of inner dogs from Activity 1.

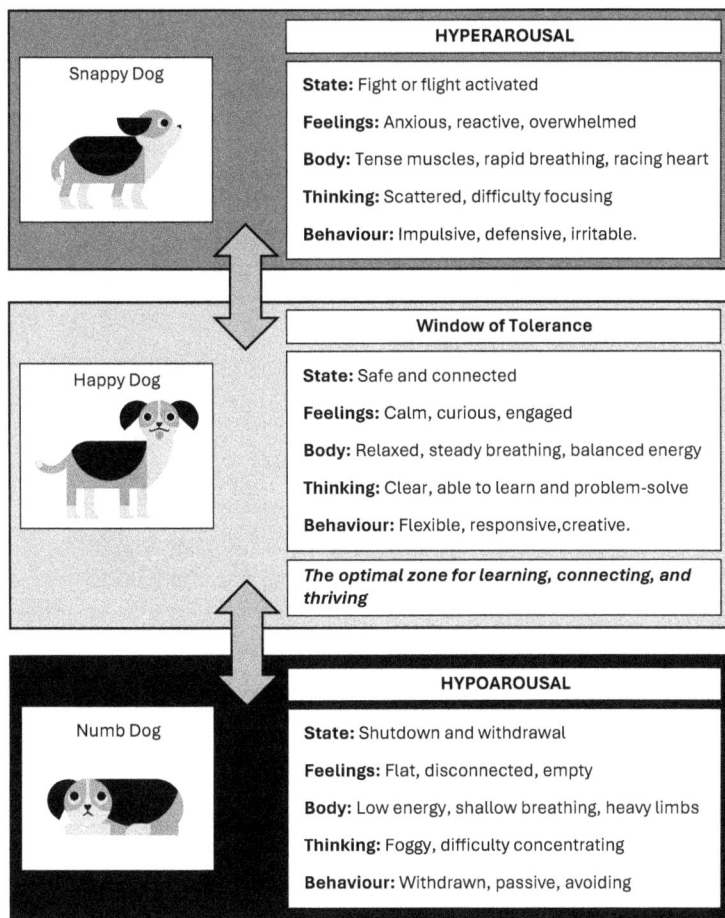

Snappy Dog	**HYPERAROUSAL**
	State: Fight or flight activated
	Feelings: Anxious, reactive, overwhelmed
	Body: Tense muscles, rapid breathing, racing heart
	Thinking: Scattered, difficulty focusing
	Behaviour: Impulsive, defensive, irritable.

Happy Dog	**Window of Tolerance**
	State: Safe and connected
	Feelings: Calm, curious, engaged
	Body: Relaxed, steady breathing, balanced energy
	Thinking: Clear, able to learn and problem-solve
	Behaviour: Flexible, responsive, creative.
	The optimal zone for learning, connecting, and thriving

Numb Dog	**HYPOAROUSAL**
	State: Shutdown and withdrawal
	Feelings: Flat, disconnected, empty
	Body: Low energy, shallow breathing, heavy limbs
	Thinking: Foggy, difficulty concentrating
	Behaviour: Withdrawn, passive, avoiding

Technique 1: The three breaths

This short grounding practice helps clients reset quickly and regain a sense of control. It can be especially useful before stressful events such as interviews or presentations.

Step 1: Getting ready

Ask your client to sit comfortably with their back supported, feet flat on the floor and ears, shoulders and hips in alignment.

Invite them to place a finger about five centimetres (two inches) below the belly button, a point known in several martial arts as the *dantian*, often described as the body's centre of energy. For those unfamiliar with it, simply describe it as a grounding point.

Step 2: Taking the breaths

Encourage them to close their eyes if safe, or to look softly down the bridge of their nose.

Guide them to imagine breathing in from the *dantian*.

Ask them to breathe in for a count of three, and out for a count of five, silently counting in their head. At the same time, talk them through each breath:

First breath: *"As you breathe out, let your shoulders, back, and knees release tension. Feel your feet safe and supported on the floor."*

Second breath: *"Notice your weight sinking into the chair, and again feel your feet grounded and secure."*

Third breath: *"Take this breath on your own. Let go of any remaining tension and notice your body supported by the seat and the floor beneath you."*

Once they have completed the three breaths, encourage them to discuss what happened and how their state has changed to embed their learning from the activity.

The three breaths technique gives clients a tool they can use anytime to return to regulation. Regular practice will build confidence and resilience.

Technique 2: Re-orienting to the present

This activity adapts orienting practice from Peter Levine's Somatic Experiencing (SE), a trauma therapy method developed over 40 years of clinical work. SE views trauma as survival responses that remain incomplete or "stuck" in the body, keeping the nervous system in states of fight, flight or freeze. Orienting restores balance by directing attention to sensory awareness:

- interoceptive (internal bodily sensations, e.g. heartbeat),
- proprioceptive (awareness of body position),
- kinaesthetic (sense of movement), and
- external sensory input.

By re-engaging these pathways, the nervous system receives signals of safety, which support regulation and presence. This aligns with wider neuroscience, including Antonio Damasio's somatic marker hypothesis, which highlights the role of bodily awareness in emotional regulation. As a practice, orienting helps clients move out of hyper- or hypo-arousal and back into their window of tolerance.

To begin the activity, ask the client to turn their head to the right slowly. Invite them to notice something in the distance that feels pleasant or interesting and notice all its qualities. Then invite them to notice something closer, still on the right.

Repeat the same process on the left side, first near, then further away.

Now, ask them to glance gently over each shoulder, noticing that nothing is behind them to cause concern.

Bring their gaze forward again and invite them to feel the edges of each of their hands, paying attention to the texture and sensation as a final grounding step.

Here are some reflection questions you could use to help the client explore further and reinforce their learning once they have completed the orienting activity:

- *"How do you feel now?"*
- *"What changed in your body?"*
- *"When might this be useful for you?"*

This simple practice equips clients with a tool they can use anytime to return to regulation. With practice, the act of orienting can expand a client's capacity to stay grounded, connected and open to learning.

Those clients who react well to this type of activity may find it helpful to explore guided visualisations and mindfulness activities. Those who are particularly auditory may also benefit from listening to ambient music.

ACTIVITY 3: USING GRATITUDE PRACTICE TO RESET FOCUS

This final activity uses gratitude journalling to develop a more positive outlook for work and life. According to Robert Emmons, a world-leading scientific expert on the topic, gratitude has two key components: it is both an affirmation of goodness and a recognition that the sources of this goodness come from outside of ourselves. Emmons also co-developed the Gratitude Questionnaire. American researcher, Barbara L Fredrickson also identified the importance of gratitude, including it as one of the 10 big positive emotions in her Broaden and Build theory of positive emotions. Meanwhile, gratitude is also one of the 24 positive psychology character strengths.

It forms part of the virtue category of *transcendence*, a group of strengths which help individuals to *"connect with the larger universe and provide meaning."*

Gratitude has been shown to offer wide-ranging benefits in four key areas:

- **Psychologically**, it boosts wellbeing, resilience, optimism and meaning.
- **Physically**, it improves immunity, sleep, exercise and overall health.
- **Socially**, it fosters generosity, forgiveness, connection and reduces loneliness.
- In **careers**, it enhances leadership, decision-making, meaning at work and reduces stress and turnover.

From a neuroscience perspective, research indicates that gratitude activates key brain regions, including the **medial prefrontal cortex**, **anterior cingulate cortex** and **hypothalamus**, key areas involved in reward, emotion regulation, learning, decision-making and stress control. Gratitude also stimulates the brain's **dopamine** reward system, boosting wellbeing and motivating positive behaviour. Over time, regular gratitude practice can reshape **neural pathways**, making the brain more responsive to positive experiences and supporting long-term mental health.

Similarly, journalling itself helps cultivate gratitude and offers additional benefits, such as reducing anxiety and depression, boosting immune function, aiding recovery from trauma and improving memory.

Gratitude journalling can help clients learn from triggers, recognise growth in setbacks and reflect on what went well. Identifying a theme and using prompts tailored to their goals and values encourages deeper engagement. The most effective prompt questions are those tailored to the client's goals and values, with space to review patterns and insights in subsequent coaching conversations. Here are some examples of journalling prompts you could use to support developing gratitude and strengthening a client's individual window of tolerance:

- *"How truly present was I today? How can I be more present tomorrow?"*
- *"What is one good thing from today that I normally take for granted?"*
- *"What experience today am I grateful for that helped me learn something important?"*

- "Where have I been able to witness my values in action and being respected today?"
- "What did I allow to steal my joy, and how can I prevent that from happening again?"
- "What element of nature did I enjoy today?"
- "What three things am I grateful for today?"

Using the same prompts consistently over several weeks helps clients build self-understanding, recognise patterns and generate insights for exploration in later coaching sessions.

Summary

Burnout, the final and most consuming of the Seven Career Thieves, represents the culmination of the patterns explored throughout this book. Unlike the earlier Thieves of Perfectionism, Comparison and Approval-Seeking, which erode wellbeing by driving clients away from authenticity, or the later Thieves of Overwhelm, Disconnection and Depletion, which strip energy, belonging and resilience, the final Thief of Burnout signals a systemic breakdown when values are compromised, and recovery is neglected. Anwen's story illustrates how exhaustion, loss of meaning and the collapse of identity can emerge from prolonged misalignment and a period of self-neglect.

Yet, as this chapter has shown, burnout also offers the possibility of renewal when clients are supported to listen to their bodies, reconnect with their values and rebuild careers in ways that honour both contribution and sustainability. Together, the Seven Thieves trace a journey from striving, through the erosion of connection and resilience, to eventual collapse in burnout. Crucially, the insights gained from identifying and understanding these thieves create a framework for restoring balance, fulfilment and long-term career wellbeing. The following concluding chapter explores what this means for career development practice in education and industry and asks the final, crucial question: how can we create conditions where achievers can flourish without falling prey to these thieves?

7. The Thief of Burnout
At a glance

Definition: "A syndrome conceptualized as resulting from chronic workplace stress that has not been successfully managed. It is characterized by three dimensions: feelings of energy depletion or exhaustion; increased mental distance from one's job, or feelings of negativism or cynicism related to one's job; and reduced professional efficacy." (WHO)

Key theories and models:

1. **Three-Dimensional Model (Maslach and Jackson, 1981):** Burnout arises through emotional exhaustion, depersonalisation (cynicism) and reduced personal accomplishment, highlighting relational strain between person and work.
2. **Areas of Worklife Model (Leiter and Maslach, 1999):** Burnout results from mismatches in workload, control, reward, community, fairness and values. Alignment across these areas fosters engagement.

Impact and context:

34% of adults experience high/extreme stress; the UK loses 16.4 million working days annually to stress/anxiety.

Highest in young adults/early career; women report higher rates due to emotional exhaustion.

Neurodivergent individuals are often at significantly higher risk due to masking and environmental mismatch.

Highest in healthcare, education, police and social work; over a third of UK entrepreneurs report severe burnout.

- **Early career:** Erodes profession intentity.
- **Mid-career:** Reduces advancement.
- **Late career:** Earlier retirement.

Warning signs:

- **Chronic exhaustion:** Persistent fatigue that rest doesn't relieve.
- **Cynicism and detachment:** Negative attitudes towards work, clients or colleagues.
- **Reduced efficacy:** Feeling incompetent and questioning work quality.
- **Values violation:** "This goes against everything I believe in."
- **Physical symptoms:** Sleep disturbances, frequent illness, headaches.
- **Emotional numbness:** Loss of joy in activities once enjoyed.
- **Self-neglect:** "I'm abandoning myself to keep everyone else comfortable."

Self-neglect through constantly prioritising work over wellbeing

3. **Demand-Control-Support Model (Karasek, 1979 and Theorell, 1990):** Stress and burnout stem from high demands combined with low control and weak social support. Balance and relationships buffer against strain.
4. **Effort-Reward Imbalance Model (Siegrist, 1996):** Burnout emerges when high work effort is met with low reward, especially in overcommitted individuals. Fairness and recognition are central to wellbeing.
5. **Existential Theory of Burnout (Pines, 1993):** Burnout results from a crisis of meaning, particularly for high achievers, when emotionally invested work fails to provide fulfilment in mission-driven roles.

Neuroscience:

Burnout produces distinct, measurable changes in brain structure and chemistry, affecting how we think, feel and function:

- **Prefrontal cortex:** Reduced activity impairs decision-making and self-regulation.
- **Amygdala:** Hyperactivity increases emotional reactivity and anxiety.
- **Hippocampus:** Atrophy affects learning, memory and adaptation to challenges.
- **HPA axis:** Disrupted stress response: high then low cortisol, weakened immunity.

Neurochemical imbalances in dopamine, serotonin, and BDNF reduce motivation, impair mood regulation and strip away normal capacity for pleasure and recovery.

Key coaching activities:

1. **Managing your Inner Dog:** Use polyvagal theory to recognise stress patterns and understand nervous system responses to workplace situations.
2. **Increasing Emotional Bandwidths:** Learn grounding techniques and orienting practices to stay balanced and maintain capacity for learning and connection.
3. **Gratitude Practice Reset:** Use structured gratitude journalling to rebuild positive neural pathways and shift focus from depletion to appreciation.

Core takeaway: Shift from **self-sacrifice** to **sustainable service and contribution**.

8 | From thieves to guardians

Building sustainable achievement

> **"Each one of us can make a difference.**
> **Together we make change."**
> Barbara Mikulski, American ex-senator and social worker.

Ensuring sustainable career success through wellbeing

Anwen's words at the end of the last chapter captured both the cost of burnout and the first step towards recovery: *"For the first time in years, I'm not abandoning myself to keep everyone else comfortable."* Her shift raised the central question of this book: How do we prevent achievers from reaching that point in the first place?

The answer lies in using our understanding of the Seven Career Thieves and how they collude to create the Seven Protection Principles. You might think of the latter as the protectors of sustainable achievement. Where the thieves steal fulfilment, the principles safeguard it, preventing relapse and building long-term resilience and sustainable growth and development.

From the very beginning, Geraldine's story showed us how perfectionism quietly takes hold. *"I have to get this right,"* she confessed, a phrase that revealed how easily the drive to excel can begin to corrode wellbeing. Perfectionism is the most common thief and often the gateway to the others.

From there, the process to burnout that affects achievers in particular unfolded. Ben admitted, *"There was always a comparison."* Amir revealed his *"fear of being a disappointment."* Charlie described the endless *"what-if"* loops of overwhelm. Ivan confessed he felt *"slow... like I'm not progressing."* Brian said, *"I feel like I'm disappearing."* And Anwen finally named the cost of it all: *"The cost of that... well, it's me."*

These voices illustrate what happens without protection.

By reversing the order of the Seven Thieves, a protective strategy is revealed that is underpinned by both theory and evidence.

Introducing the Seven Protection Principles

The Seven Protection Principles provide a framework for creating conditions where achievers can flourish without falling prey to the thieves. Together, they provide a foundation-building sequence and career development strategy designed to prevent achievers, in particular, from developing the very vulnerabilities which, left unchecked, can end in burnout.

Think of them as the Seven Guardians – practical capacities to cultivate with clients and within workplaces – to create:

1. **Sustainable Self-Care**
   - Protects against the Thief of Burnout by safeguarding energy through rest, renewal and healthy boundaries.

2. **Purpose and Belonging**
   - Protects against the Thief of Disconnection by anchoring achievement in meaning and trusted relationships.

3. **Aligned Energy**
   - Protects against the Thief of Depletion by managing energy though aligning values-led strengths, talents and skills.

4. **Clarity of Focus**
   - Protects against the Thief of Overwhelm by prioritising what matters most and setting appropriate boundaries with confidence.

5. **Authentic Self-Direction**
   - Protects against the Thief of Comparison by valuing the self and the unique qualities an individual has so they can walk their own path with confidence.

6. **Unique Contribution**
   - Protects against the Thief of Comparison by valuing yourself and the unique qualities you have so you can walk your own path with confidence.

7. **Self-Compassionate Mastery**
   - Protects against the Thief of Perfectionism by seeking excellence through valuing growth, learning and above all, kindness to self.

Combined with the Seven Career Thieves diagnostic lens and the chapter-based activities, the Seven Protection Principles (referred to as Guardians with clients) form a three-part methodology:

- **Assessment** – spotting the thieves that are active, whether through conversation, reflection or diagnostic tools.
- **Intervention** – supporting clients, students or employees with targeted strategies that address the patterns already at work.
- **Prevention** – embedding the Protection Principles to build sustainable habits and systems that reduce recurrence.

A new diagnostic for career wellbeing

To support practitioners in applying the Seven Career Thieves and Protection Principles with clients, the Sustainable Career Success Profile is available on the Career Alchemy website (www.careeralchemy.co.uk). You can also access the link, along with other book resources, via the QR code or the web address provided at the start of this book.

This evidence-based diagnostic tool provides an overview of which thieves are most active and which Protection Principles need strengthening, supporting targeted intervention and prevention planning in a confidential and data-compliant way.

Practitioners can use it as a triage tool to focus discussion and coaching sessions and to track progress over time, while clients gain immediate insights to reflect on before career wellbeing coaching begins.

Recommendations for professional practice

For ease, the following considerations are grouped by professional role. Rather than being prescriptive checklists, please think of them more as prompts to consider how you can use the Seven Thieves and the Seven Protection Principles in your own practice and organisational context.

For career development professionals

- Remember to look for indicators of the Seven Career Thieves in action when hearing client stories.
- Refer when your professional judgement recognises that careers support alone is insufficient and a therapeutic referral may be required.
- Consider bringing a wellbeing lens into assessments by including questions about stress, striving, happiness and success and challenging any conflicting ideas or behaviours.
- Explain the Seven Career Thieves and Protection Principles frameworks to ensure that clients are appropriately scaffolded on their journey and can progress effectively.
- Consider tracking client outcomes holistically to reinforce progress, given that, as we know, improved wellbeing and confidence matter as much as career milestones as career enablers.
- In practice: ask reflective questions (*"How do you usually respond when plans don't work out?"*), use diagnostic tools such as the

Sustainable Career Success Profile tool for triage, and provide reframes and activities that encourage new ways of thinking that work for achievers.

For executive coaches

- Consider using the Seven Career Thieves and Protection Principles framework to work proactively with high-potential leaders who may be at risk of derailment through perfectionism or burnout.
- Explore with clients whether their organisational culture rewards unhealthy striving and how they might influence change.
- Create reflective spaces, individually or in teams, where leaders can talk honestly about the costs of achievement.
- Encourage the use of practical tools such as values and excellence-led decision-making with clients to help them reframe perfectionism effectively.
- Encourage energy and stress-response mapping so executives can recognise early signs of overwhelm and the onset of depletion for themselves.

For careers educators

- Introduce the Seven Career Thieves and Protection Principles into careers education so learners understand how to achieve without sacrificing their wellbeing.
- Support teachers and advisers to notice perfectionist, comparison, approval-seeking, and overwhelm tendencies in students and intervene early.
- Pay special attention to transition points (e.g. GCSE to A level, university entry, graduation), when achievement pressures peak.
- Use reflective activities such as the Life Values Compass to help learners link career goals and social media use with authentic personal meaning.
- Reframe assessment as feedback for growth rather than measures of worth and encourage peer mentoring to build healthy achievement habits.

For HR professionals

- Consider how recruitment and performance management systems can distinguish between healthy achievement and perfectionist overdrive.
- Reward sustainable excellence and learning rather than short-term productivity above all else, wherever possible.
- Shape career pathways that explicitly balance contribution with self-care.

- Provide training for line managers to recognise and respond constructively when employees push themselves beyond healthy limits.
- Review existing policies and revise them so they support the Seven Protection Principles where needed to remove roadblocks to health, productivity and engagement that may lead to grievances, severance and court cases.
- Review exit interview data for evidence of burnout or perfectionism contributing to attrition, and use the insights to help inform culture change.

Implementation framework

The Seven Protection Principles work best when practitioners help clients build them as interconnected habits rather than isolated skills. Starting with one guardian principle and gradually expanding ensures that clients create sustainable change that they can maintain long-term.

By embedding the Protection Principles in this way, practitioners, educators, coaches and HR leaders can create ecosystems of support. The framework is more than simply a set of tools; it is a methodology for preventing the achievement trap, protecting talent and cultivating careers that last despite a constantly changing economy

Embedding the guardian principles gradually ensures that change sticks, protecting against the yo-yo effect where progress unravels once immediate pressures ease.

Closing reflections

The journey through this book has traced the arc from vulnerability to protection: from the Seven Career Thieves that quietly erode fulfilment, to the Seven Protection Principles that safeguard sustainable achievement. Together, they form a methodology that blends assessment, intervention and prevention, giving practitioners, educators, coaches and HR leaders a way to support achievers that is both evidence-based and humane.

By combining assessment, intervention and prevention, we can build career wellbeing in cultures where success is not only possible but sustainable.

As you bring these insights into your own context and practice, remember that small shifts create lasting change – whether a reframed belief, a newly drawn boundary or a values-led choice. When multiplied across classrooms, coaching sessions, workplaces and boardrooms, these shifts can create cultures that are resilient, hopeful, kind and innovative and places where achievement and human potential can flourish and grow regardless of constant change.

In the words of the American author, educator and activist, Parker J. Palmer:

> *Our deepest calling is to grow into our own authentic self-hood, whether or not it conforms to some image of who we ought to be. As we do so, we will not only find the joy that every human being seeks – we will also find our path of authentic service in the world.*

Appendix

Key theory summaries

Introduction

Here is an overview of the influential theories and concepts which run through this book.

Theory of Needs (Three Needs Theory) (McClelland, 1961)

This theory identifies three key motivators, achievement, affiliation and power, that drive workplace behaviour. Individuals' dominant needs influence goal-setting, leadership style, decision-making and satisfaction, shaping performance and organisational culture.

Acceptance and Commitment Therapy (ACT) (Hayes, 1999)

ACT promotes psychological flexibility by encouraging acceptance of difficult thoughts, mindfulness of the present and commitment to values-based actions, reducing avoidance and fostering resilience, wellbeing and authentic living.

Self-Compassion Theory (Neff, 2003)

Self-compassion involves treating oneself with kindness, recognising shared humanity and practising mindful awareness, fostering resilience, emotional balance and reduced self-criticism compared to perfectionistic or harsh self-judgement.

Hope Action Theory (Niles, Amundson and Yoon 2010)

Hope Action Theory integrates positive psychology with action-oriented career strategies across six competencies: self-reflection, self-clarity, visioning, goal-setting, implementing adaptable action and feedback learning to build fulfilling careers.

Mindfulness-Based Stress Reduction (MBSR) (Kabat-Zinn, 1979)

MBSR is a structured eight-week, evidence-based programme developed by Jon Kabat-Zinn that uses mindfulness meditation and gentle yoga to reduce stress, enhance self-awareness and promote emotional and physical wellbeing.

Expressive Writing Paradigm (James Pennebaker, 1986)

Journalling theory suggests expressive writing promotes health and wellbeing by enabling emotional disclosure, cognitive processing and meaning-making, helping individuals regulate emotions, reduce stress and integrate difficult experiences into coherent personal narratives.

Chapter 1: The Thief of Perfectionism

Self-Discrepancy Theory (Higgins, 1987)

This theory explains perfectionism as distress arising from gaps between actual, ideal and ought-selves, with unmet aspirations or obligations driving chronic striving, anxiety and dissatisfaction.

Frost Multidimensional Perfectionism Scale (Frost et al., 1990)

This theory defines perfectionism through six dimensions: mistakes, standards, parental influence, doubts and organisation, highlighting how family and cognitive factors create achievement pressure and heightened anxiety.

Multidimensional Perfectionism Scale (Hewitt and Flett, 1991)

This model identifies self-oriented, other-oriented and socially prescribed perfectionism, showing how high internal standards and external expectations interact to heighten vulnerability to stress, self-criticism and strained relationships.

Clinical Perfectionism Model (Shafran, Cooper and Fairburn, 2002)

This model frames perfectionism as achievement-dependent self-worth, where biased evaluation and negative self-talk maintain unrealistic standards and relentless striving despite harmful personal consequences.

Positive Strivings versus Negative Concerns (Stoeber and Otto, 2006)

This theory distinguishes adaptive perfectionist strivings from maladaptive concerns, showing how high standards can foster achievement but excessive worry about mistakes fuels anxiety, depression and low self-esteem.

2 × 2 Model of Perfectionism (Gaudreau and Thompson, 2010)

This theory shows how personal standards and evaluative concerns combine to form adaptive or maladaptive perfectionism profiles, with mixed types carrying the greatest risk for stress and burnout.

Chapter 2: The Thief of Comparison

Social Comparison Theory (Festinger, 1954)

This theory explains how people evaluate themselves by comparing with others, where upward comparisons can inspire growth but also fuel inadequacy, envy and diminished self-esteem.

Self-Evaluation Maintenance Theory (SEM) (Tesser, 1988)

This theory shows how another's success boosts self-esteem in irrelevant domains but threatens it in valued ones, with closeness, relevance and performance shaping the comparison's impact.

Perceived Fraudulence Theory/Imposter Phenomenon (Clance and Imes, 1978)

This theory describes persistent self-doubt and perceived fraudulence despite success, linking imposter feelings to perfectionism, comparison, overwork and fear of exposure in competitive environments.

Prospect Theory (Kahneman and Tversky, 1979)

This theory shows how people judge outcomes relative to reference points, with losses weighing more than gains, magnifying comparative setbacks and fuelling risk-averse decision-making.

Relative Deprivation Theory (Stouffer, 1949)

This theory highlights how feelings of disadvantage arise from comparisons with slightly better-off peers, where subjective inequality fuels dissatisfaction, resentment and disengagement.

Chapter 3: The Thief of Approval-Seeking

Social Influence Theory (Kelman, 1953/1958)

This theory explains how behaviour shifts through compliance, identification or internalisation, showing how people adapt to gain approval or avoid rejection under social pressure.

Attachment Theory (Bowlby, 1969; Ainsworth, 1978)

This theory shows how insecure attachment styles shape adult approval-seeking, with anxious and avoidant patterns fuelling people-pleasing, fear of rejection and dependence on external validation.

Social Learning Theory (Bandura, 1977)

This theory explains how approval-seeking is learnt through modelling, imitation, and vicarious reinforcement (observing others' behaviours being rewarded or punished), encouraging individuals to pursue external validation for safety, belonging, and social acceptance.

Self-Determination Theory (Deci and Ryan, 1985-present)

This theory proposes that autonomy, competence and relatedness underpin motivation, with unmet needs increasing reliance on external validation and fulfilled needs fostering authentic engagement.

Schema Theory (Young, 1990s)

This theory highlights how unmet childhood needs create maladaptive approval-seeking schemas, where validation is prioritised over authenticity, driving people-pleasing, anxiety and inauthentic choices.

Chapter 4: The Thief of Overwhelm

Stress Appraisal and Coping Theory (Lazarus and Folkman, 1984)

This theory explains how overwhelm arises from how individuals interpret demands and evaluate their coping resources, with responses shaped by perceived threat, available support and ongoing reappraisal.

Cognitive Load Theory (Sweller, 1988)

In this theory, Sweller proposes that overwhelm occurs when information or mental effort exceeds working memory capacity, distinguishing between intrinsic, extraneous and germane loads that affect learning and performance.

Person-Environment Fit (P-E Fit) Theory (University of Michigan research team inc. Caplan, van Harrison, Kahn, French, late 1970s)

P-E Fit theory suggests that overwhelm results from a mismatch between a person's abilities or needs and the demands or resources of their environment, particularly as subjectively perceived.

Demand-Control-Support (DCS) Model (Karasek (1979) extended by Theorell and Johnson in late 1980s)

This theory posits that overwhelm peaks when high demands combine with low control and minimal support, making autonomy and social support essential buffers against stress and burnout.

Job Demands-Resources (JD-R) Model
(Demerouti and Bakker, 2001)

The JD-R Model explains that overwhelm emerges when job demands outweigh available resources, leading to exhaustion and disengagement – unless buffered by personal strengths like resilience, optimism and self-efficacy.

Chapter 5: The Thief of Depletion

Ego Depletion Theory (Strength or Resource Model)
(Baumeister et al., 1998)

This theory posits that self-control draws on limited mental resources that get depleted with use, reducing willpower, focus and persistence, until recovery through rest or motivation restores capacity.

Conservation of Resources (COR) Theory (Hobfoll, 1989ff)

COR theory explains stress and burnout as resulting from the loss or threatened loss of personal, social or material resources that individuals strive to protect, maintain and restore.

Action Regulation Theory (ART) (Hacker and Frese, 2017)

ART explains how people plan, execute and adjust goal-directed behaviour through cognitive regulation, highlighting how task complexity, self-monitoring and poor work design can increase mental strain and depletion.

Allostatic Load Theory (McEwen and Stellar, 1993; McEwen, 1998)

This theory explains how chronic stress accumulates biological "wear and tear," weakening the brain and body's regulation systems and increasing risk of burnout, disease and emotional depletion without proper recovery.

Emotional Labour Theory (Hochschild, 1983; Grandey, 2000)

This theory explains how workers manage emotions to meet job demands. Surface acting (faking emotions) leads to emotional dissonance and depletion, while deep acting (genuine feeling) is less harmful, and better still, authentic emotions and their expression require no effort at all.

Chapter 6: The Thief of Disconnection

Logotherapy (Frankl, 1946/1959)

Frankl's work explains psychological distress as stemming from a loss of meaning. When individuals cannot connect work or life to a deeper purpose, they may experience apathy, identity erosion or disengagement.

Recognition Theory (Honneth, 1992)

This theory proposes that self-worth develops through being seen, valued and affirmed. When recognition is denied across personal, legal or social spheres, disconnection and identity disruption occur.

Attachment Theory (Bowlby, 1969; Ainsworth, 1978; Hasan and Shaver, 1987)

This theory explains how early bonding patterns shape emotional regulation and workplace connection. Insecure attachment increases risk of disconnection through relational avoidance, mistrust or emotional dysregulation.

Social Identity Theory (SIT) (Tajfel and Turner, 1979)

SIT describes how self-esteem and belonging depend on group membership. Threats to identity from exclusion or marginalisation can lead to disconnection, withdrawal or reduced professional engagement.

Ecological Systems Theory (Bronfenbrenner, 1979)

This theory views disconnection as arising from misalignment across nested systems: individual, relational, organisational, cultural or societal, highlighting how context, not just mindset, shapes career engagement.

Chapter 7: The Thief of Burnout

Three-Dimensional Theory (Maslach and Jackson, 1981)

This seminal theory outlines how burnout arises through emotional exhaustion, depersonalisation (cynicism) and reduced personal accomplishment. It highlights the relational strain between the person and their work, rather than casting burnout as an individual weakness.

Areas of Worklife Model (Leiter and Maslach, 1999)

This theory builds on Maslach's original theory. It highlights that burnout results from mismatches in workload, control, reward, community, fairness and values; alignment across these areas fosters engagement, while misfit accelerates exhaustion and disengagement.

Demand-Control-Support (DCS) Model (Karasek, 1979, extended by Theorell, 1990)

This theory identifies stress and burnout as stemming from high demands combined with low control and weak social support, indicating that balance and supportive relationships are needed to buffer against strain and foster resilience.

Effort-Reward Imbalance (ERI) Model (Siegrist, 1996)

This theory indicates that burnout emerges when high work effort is met with low reward, especially in overcommitted individuals; fairness and recognition are central to wellbeing and motivation.

Existential Theory of Burnout (Pines, 1993, 2000)

In this theory, burnout is identified as the result of a crisis of meaning, particularly for high achievers, which arises when emotionally invested work fails to provide fulfilment, particularly in mission-driven roles where purpose and values are central.

Chapter 8: From thieves to guardians

The Sustainable Career Success Profile (Parry, 2025)

An evidence-based diagnostic tool for career practitioners, coaches, educators and HR professionals to assess sustainable career success and support interventions using the Seven Career Thieves and Protection Principles framework.

www.ingramcontent.com/pod-product-compliance
Lightning Source LLC
Chambersburg PA
CBHW060304220326
41598CB00027B/4228